ENDORSEMENTS

"These pages by Pastor Delores R. Medley unfold spiritual truths concerning love and particularly truths about Father God's love for the hearts of men as demonstrated by the life of our Lord and Savior Jesus Christ. This pocketbook of Scriptures contains vital information and inspiration for all who will devote themselves to its words. As Delores' pastor for the past eighteen years, I wholeheartedly endorse her and this book. It's for such a time as this. As you read and meditate on these writings, take the time to let the truths from Father God's Word saturate you wholly—spirit, soul, and body. Allow the Lord to minister to you and fill you with His love. Such is His aim and destiny for your life."

Darryl W. Medley, Senior Pastor
Spirit and Truth United Church of Worship Albemarle, NC
Vision Hope and Peace United Church of Worship Lenoir, NC

"I, with excitement, endorse *Love's Aim*. Delores Medley, the author, carries a "love mantle" and knows exactly how to set it down in the midst of enemy strongholds which block the operation of gifts and spiritual identities in the Body of Christ. I have witnessed her "love mantle" change mindsets and set captive saints free. What Delores walks in is life-changing! Read her book!"

Pamela Smith
Aglow International, President Western North Carolina Aglow Area,
Mid-Atlantic Region, Statesville, NC

"*Love's Aim* is a devotional filled with Scriptures that express the aims of God via His love. Author Delores Medley is a true woman of God who not only writes about God's love, but walks in true love, lives true love, and shows true love. She demonstrates God's love here on earth in the flesh. Agape love involves faithfulness, commitment, and an act of the will. It is distinguished from other types of love by its lofty moral nature and strength of character. 1 Corinthians 13 beautifully describes this agape love, and Delores showers such love on everyone. As you read the pages of *Love's Aim*, you will learn to love as never before, because the love of God that pours through Delores will flow to you from its pages. Get ready; get set; and go love!"

Sharean B. Williams
Sharean's House of Bethany prayer house, Albemarle, North Carolina

"I've known Minister Delores Medley for some years now. I can say she truly personifies the love of God, and she is ever willing to share that love with all."

Minister Argene Peoples
Shiloh Baptist Church, Badin, North Carolina

"It's been my honor to know Delores very intimately as her hair stylist for the past fifteen years. She reminds others of God's love and faithfulness. Delores relies on the Holy Spirit as her cornerstone, and God's love shines through her. Her faith sustained her when she faced family heartache and sorrow. And she has prayed over me when I did not know what to pray for or was too hurt to pray at all. Delores has guided me as a spiritual mother. I have watched her love those shunned by others; I have heard her minister to hurting people. Delores is an inspiration who lifts up every person who crosses her path. I am excited about Delores' release of this daily devotional as I don't know anyone more devoted to the Trinity or God's Word of love. May all her readers be blessed."

Gerald's Hair Center and Day Spa
Albemarle, North Carolina

LOVE'S AIM

A DEVOTIONAL

Delores Roseboro Medley

LOVE'S AIM
Copyright © 2017 Delores Roseboro Medley
All Rights Reserved

All Rights Reserved. This book was published by lulu.com for Delores Roseboro Medley. No part of this book may be reproduced in any form by any means without the express written permission of the author. This includes reprints, excerpts, photocopying, recording, or any future means of reproducing text.

Scriptures marked (AMPC) are taken from the Amplified® Bible (AMPC), Copyright © 1954, 1958, 1962, 1964, 1965, 1987 by The Lockman Foundation Used by permission. www.Lockman.org

Scripture quotations marked NASB are taken from the *New American Standard Bible*, Copyright 1960, 1962, 1963, 1968, 1971, 1972, 1973, 1975, 1977, 1995 by The Lockman Foundation. Used by permission.

Scriptures marked (TLV) are taken from the Tree of Life (TLV) Translation of the Bible. Copyright © 2015 by The Messianic Jewish Family Bible Society. Baker Publishing Group. Used by permission.

Scriptures marked (RcV) are taken from the Recovery Version. Copyright © 1985, 1991 Living Stream Ministry. Used by permission.

Scriptures marked (NTE) taken from The New Testament for Everyone and the copyright is © Nicholas Thomas Wright 2011. Used by permission.

Scripture quotations marked NIV are taken from the *Holy Bible, New International Version. NIV.* Copyright 1973, 1978, 1984 by International Bible Society. Used by permission of Zondervan. All rights reserved.

Scripture quotations marked TLB are taken from *The Living Bible* copyright 1971. Used by permission of Tyndale House Publishers, Inc., Carol Stream, Illinois 60188. All rights reserved.

Scripture quotations marked NLT are taken from the *Holy Bible, New Living Translation*, copyright 1996, 2004, 2007. Used by permission of Tyndale House Publishers, Inc. Carol Stream, Illinois 60188. All rights reserved.

Scriptures marked (EXB) THE EXPANDED BIBLE are taken from the THE EXPANDED BIBLE (The Expanded Bible): Copyright© 2011 by Thomas Nelson, Inc. Used by permission. All rights reserved.

Scriptures marked (ESV) are taken from *The Holy Bible,* English Standard Version *(ESV).* Copyright 2001 by Crossway Bibles, a division of Good News Publishers. Used by permission. All rights reserved.

Scriptures marked (VOICE) are taken from The Voice™. Copyright© 2008 by Ecclesia Bible Society. Used by permission. All rights reserved.

Scripture quotations marked KJV are from the Holy Bible, King James Version (Authorized Version). First published in 1611. Quoted from the KJV Classic Reference Bible, Copyright 1983 by The Zondervan Corporation.

Scripture quotations marked NKJV are taken from the New King James Version. Copyright 1982 by Thomas Nelson, Inc. Used by permission. All rights reserved.

Scripture quotations marked HCSB are from the Holman Christian Standard Bible. HCSB. Copyright 1999, 2000, 2002, 2003 by Holman Bible Publishers. Used by permission. Holman Christian Standard Bible, Holman CSB, and HCSB are federally registered trademarks of Holman Bible Publishers.

Scripture quotations marked MSG are taken from The Message. Copyright 1993, 1994, 1995, 1996, 2000, 2001, 2002, 2003 by Eugene H. Peterson. Used by permission of NavPress Publishing Group.

Scriptures marked (CJB) are taken from the COMPLETE JEWISH BIBLE (CJB): copyright© 1998 by David H. Stern. Published by Jewish New Testament Publications, Inc. www.messianicjewish.net/ jntp. Distributed by Messianic Jewish Resources Int'l. www.messianicjewish.net. All rights reserved. Used by permission.

Scripture quotations marked Phillips are from The New Testament in Modern English, Copyright © 1958, 1959, 1960, 1972 J. B. Phillips.

Scriptures marked (CEB) are taken from the Common English Bible®, CEB® Copyright © 2010, 2011 by Common English Bible™. Used by permission. All rights reserved worldwide.

If you would like permission to use any part of *Love's Aim*, please contact Assistant Pastor Delores Roseboro Medley at Spirit and Truth United Church of Worship, 100 Moss Springs Road, Albemarle, NC 28001.

Editing by Katherine Bell, katherinefbell@me.com
Typesetting by Sally Hanan, www.inksnatcher.com
Cover art by Ellen Bell Holland, ebholland@icloud.com
Cover design by Amy Hathcock, aghathcock@gmail.com

Love's Aim/Delores Roseboro Medley. —1st ed.
ISBN 978-1-387-51659-9

God's love is perfect, faithful, unconditional, forgiving, all-encompassing, pure, lasting, and ever present. His love has moved me to write Love's Aim.

I dedicate the journey of producing Love's Aim to my loving family and the memory of my beloved brother Michael Glenn Roseboro, the one who left too soon.

God covenants in Jeremiah 31:3: "Yes, I have loved you with an everlasting love; therefore with loving-kindness have I drawn you and continued My faithfulness to you." (AMPC)

CONTENTS

SECTION ONE..1
LOVE DEFINED

SECTION TWO..21
THE ENTRANCE OF HIS LOVE

SECTION THREE..53
LOVE SEARCHES THE HEART

SECTION FOUR..83
UNRESERVED LOVE

FOR LEADERS..101

FOREWORD

For most of my life as a Spirit-filled Christian, I've seen arrows, swords, and targets in the spirit. I am a seer, and I've seen these images while soaking in the presence of God. Many times I have ministered God's love to others as a woman of the Scripture Isaiah 49:2. The verse reads: "And He has made my mouth like a sharp sword; in the shadow of His hand has He hid me and made me a polished arrow; in His quiver has He kept me close and concealed me." (AMPC) And I've shared the promise of Ezekiel 36:26: "A new heart will I give you and a new spirit will I put within you, and I will take away the stony heart out of your flesh and give you a heart of flesh." (AMPC) I've spoken 1 John 4:16 over souls: "And so we know and rely on the love God has for us. God is love. Whoever lives in love lives in God, and God in them." (NIV)

Arrows were powerful weapons in Biblical times. They were long range weapons that hit targets hundreds of yards away. Several parts made up the composite bow and arrows, and this type required a higher level of skill and bodily control than the simple bow and arrow. The parallel is the higher maturity level it takes to walk out love to its full height and depth and width.

Also, the arrows were marked to identify ownership. I ask, "Do people look at you and know that you belong to Jesus Christ?" John 13:35 states, "By this shall all [men] know that you are My disciples, if you love one another [if you keep on showing love among yourselves]." (AMPC)

When an arrow is being formed, the shaft is placed in the quiver—a type of the secret place. Over time the maker can see whether the body of the arrow will remain straight or warp. Improperly formed arrows will not fly true. Manufacturing arrows involves an extensive process, but every step is necessary to ensure that when the archer releases the arrow, it goes where he directs. And the archer or the one in control is a type of the Lord Jesus Christ.

When the maker, a type of our Maker, places the tip on the arrow and his feathers on the shaft, the arrow can go the distance and soar to the intended destination. When you have His love, you will hit the mark. Arrows, like saints, are fashioned to hit a specific target. They are never launched haphazardly into wide open spaces in hopes they'll hit something. Arrows are released to intentionally penetrate a primary target. Saints filled with love are to intentionally influence the hearts of men.

As you read this book, may God reveal His heart to your heart. His heart burns with an amazing love for you. And God is the power behind His arrows. He is also the *dunamis* power that goes before. He takes aim at hearts with His love. May these writings—arrows of His love—hit the target of your heart and fulfill His purposes.

SECTION ONE

LOVE DEFINED

God is love all the time. He never changes. And He is good all the time. Never is there a moment in your life when God isn't full of longing to do for you all that you need Him to do. But it is your faith that opens the door for Him to do it. Faith is your connection to the love of God; you must believe the Love!

The more I study the love of God, the more I realize His love is the bottom line. When you're trusting in His love and operating by it, every spiritual principle works in your favor. When you're believing and receiving God's love and walking in it, you simply can't help but be blessed. 1 Corinthians 16:14 instructs: "Let all that you do be done in love." (NASB)

You could spend a lifetime on love, and never come to the end of it, because as a subject, it is inexhaustible. The subject of love is as big as God Himself because God is love. See 1 John 4:8. And God's love is, without question, the primary emphasis of the New Testament. It is the center of Christianity. It is the key that causes every other spiritual principle to work in your life. Know as you read this section, it's impossible to overemphasize love

AGAPE LOVE

Agape love is always shown by what it does. God displays His love most clearly at the cross. You did not deserve such a sacrifice.

> *"You see, at just the right time, when we were still powerless, Christ died for the ungodly. Very rarely will anyone die for a righteous person, though for a good person someone might possibly dare to die. But God demonstrates His own love for us in this: While we were still sinners, Christ died for us." Romans 5:6–8 NIV*

God's agape love is unmerited, gracious, and constantly seeking to benefit the ones He loves. The Bible says you are an undeserving recipient of His lavish agape love. God sacrificed His Son in a demonstration of agape love. Ephesians 2:4–8 reveals

> *"But God is so rich in mercy; he loved us so much that even though we were spiritually dead and doomed by our sins, he gave us back our lives again when he raised Christ from the dead—only by his undeserved favor have we ever been saved—and lifted us up from the grave into glory along with Christ, where we sit with him in the heavenly realms—all because of what Christ Jesus did. And now God can always point to us as examples of how very, very rich his kindness is, as shown in all he has done for us through Jesus Christ. Because of his kindness, you have been saved through trusting Christ. And even trusting is not of yourselves; it too is a gift from God." (TLB)*

Grace is getting what you do not deserve. Justice is getting what you do deserve. Mercy is not getting what you do deserve. The Word says God is so rich in mercy, and this mercy is released because of His great love. "Great love," the apostle Paul says. God's love to any degree would have been enough. God is not miserly. He withholds not His best from you who deserves nothing at all. Amazing love, indeed it is.

~Confession~

Let us look upon every brother who tries or vexes us, as God's means of grace, God's instrument for our purification, for our exercise of the humility Jesus our Life breathes within us. And let us have such faith in the All of God, and the nothing of self, that, as nothing in our own eyes, we may, in God's power, only seek to serve one another in love.

— From *Humility* by Andrew Murray

EXTRAVAGANT LOVE

1 John 3:1–3 reads

> *"See what great love the Father has lavished on us, that we should be called children of God! And that is what we are! The reason the world does not know us is that it did not know him. Dear friends, now we are children of God, and what we will be has not yet been made known. But we know that when Christ appears, we shall be like him, for we shall see him as he is. All who have this hope in him purify themselves, just as he is pure."*

The passage speaks of what manner of love the Father has lavished on you. His love is extravagant and generous. God lavishly or profusely gives love. His love is an incredible love in that He calls you one of His sons or daughters.

Beloved, you are here and now one of God's children. It is not yet clear what you will be hereafter. But when He comes and is obviously revealed, you will resemble Him. You will be like Him. And you, as one of His children, will see Him just as He really is. So now you have hope resting on you—a hope that purifies you as He is pure.

~Prayer~

Lord, thank You for Your generous love. Thank You for sending Jesus so I might experience Your incredible love today and forever. In His name: Jesus.

LOVE IS WHO HE IS

Have you ever had a sense of wonder about God's love for His people and His love for the lost and dying in the world around you? Love is not something God does; it is who He is. God is love 1 John 4:8 declares. And when you dwell in love, you dwell in God and God in you.

> *"'My sheep hear My voice, and I know them, and they follow Me.'" 1 (John 4:16)*

His love endures; it outlasts anything and everything. Imagine that! You are at your best when you love like God loves. You resemble Him. You are complete in His love. Love causes all things to fall in place with nothing missing and nothing broken.

~Prayer~

Lord, I open my heart this day to receive Your love. I receive the greatest thing in life as I receive Your love. Thank You that Your love is complete and unfailing. It endures forever. Amen.

GIFT OF LOVE

God loves you! God wants you to see and know and believe and feel that He loves you. First of all, love is an action and not just an emotional feeling. The new birth is a gift of love. Matthew 6:10 says,

> *"Every good and perfect gift is from above, coming down from the Father of the heavenly lights, who does not change like shifting shadows. He chose to give us birth through the word of truth, that we might be a kind of firstfruits of all he created." (NIV)*

His faithfulness is a gift of love. God assures you in Psalm 100:5, "For the Lord is good and his love endures forever; his faithfulness continues through all generations." (NIV) This verse not only tells of God's goodness and love but says it continues into today. God is faithful through all generations.

God's love is perfect. And receiving this perfect gift begins with faith. When you receive His gift of love, you have unexplainable peace and joy. In His love, you have confidence in the worst of situations. Often by the Spirit, it's as if you can feel His loving arms around you when you need comfort, protection, or relief from anxiety. It is by God's love that fear, worry, and the pain of rejection leave. This reality is something the unbelieving world cannot understand.

The second letter to the Corinthians ends with "Finally, brothers and sisters, rejoice! Strive for full restoration, encourage one another, be of one mind, live in peace. And the God of love and peace will be with you." (2 Corinthians 13:11 NIV)

1 John 3:1 tells of the reality of the children of God:

> "See what great love the Father has lavished on us, that we should be called children of God! And that is what we are! The reason the world does not know us is that it did not know him" (NIV)

Selah which means pause and think on that!

~P<small>RAYER</small>~

Father, help me to receive Your love and peace into my heart today. Help me to believe fully in Your love—Your perfect love. For You are good from generation to generation. You are faithful and enduring in Your love for me today. I receive love from You that breaks yokes of pain, fear, and worry. Thank You, now. In Jesus' name.

THE FATHER'S HEARTBEAT

God's heart beats with love for man. The Father has a house where there is a place prepared for you and me. The Lord went away to prepare a place for you. When He left, He promised to be with His followers in the form of the precious Holy Spirit He'd send to live inside each of them.

Come after love; pursue it. To understand the meaning of love involves a lifelong aim. Love's purpose is to lead you on the path of righteousness. Hear the voice of love beckoning you to come closer to the Father and listen to the His heartbeat. Follow the sound of this heartbeat. It will lead to the fulfillment of life and godliness.

~P<small>RAYER</small>~

Lord, help me to follow after You today. Help me to listen to the voice of Your love. May I hear the heartbeat of Your love for me and others today. In Jesus' name.

UNCONDITIONAL

1 John 4:9–10 declares,

> "This is how God showed his love among us: He sent his one and only Son into the world that we might live through him. This is love: not that we loved God, but that he loved us and sent his Son as an atoning sacrifice for our sins." (NIV)

God's love is a love that initiates; it is never merely a response. It's precisely the reality that God initiates love toward you that makes it unconditional. If God's love were conditional, then you would have to do something first to earn it or merit it, You would have to somehow appease His wrath and cleanse yourself of your sins before God could love you. But conditional love is not the Biblical message. The Biblical message or Gospel is that God, motivated by love, moved without requiring any conditions to save people from their sinful state.

Romans 5:8 says, "But God demonstrates His own love toward us, in that while we were yet sinners, Christ died for us." (NASB) And Ephesians 2 gives even more light on the subject of God's love for sinners.

> "But God is so rich in mercy and loves us with such intense love that, even when we were dead because of our acts of disobedience, he brought us to life along with the Messiah—it is by grace that you have been delivered." (Ephesians 2:4–5 CJB)

Colossians 1:13–14 paints a picture of rescue: "For he has rescued us from the dominion of darkness and brought us into the kingdom of the Son he loves, in whom we have redemption, the forgiveness of sins."

For Christ to be the head of a body of redeemed people and for His believers to be members of His body, God had to deliver souls out from under the authority of darkness and transfer them into the kingdom under

Jesus Christ. This deliverance qualifies you to partake of Christ, the all-inclusive Savior who is everything, and gain your allotted portion in Him.

~Prayer~

Father, thank You for transferring me out of the darkness into Your light. Your mercy endures forever because of Your great love for me. May my love for You exceed the love I have for any other person. I ask for more light to come into my heart concerning Your love. In Jesus' name.

BOUNDLESS

As a believer, do you really understand the mighty depths of God's love for you? The apostle Paul prayed fervently that the Ephesians would see and understand the width and length and depth and height of God's love for them. He prayed they would be rooted and grounded in that boundless love.

Meditate on Ephesians 3:14–19

> *"For this reason [seeing the greatness of this plan by which you are built together in Christ], I bow my knees before the Father of our Lord Jesus Christ, For Whom every family in heaven and on earth is named [that Father from Whom all fatherhood takes its title and derives its name]. May He grant you out of the rich treasury of His glory to be strengthened and reinforced with mighty power in the inner man by the [Holy] Spirit [Himself indwelling your innermost being and personality]. May Christ through your faith [actually] dwell (settle down, abide, make His permanent home) in your hearts! May you be rooted deep in love and founded securely on love, that you may have the power and be strong to apprehend and grasp with all the saints [God's devoted people, the experience of that love] what is the breadth and length and height and depth [of it]; [That you may really come] to know [practically, through*

> *experience for yourselves] the love of Christ, which far surpasses mere knowledge [without experience]; that you may be filled [through all your being] unto all the fullness of God [may have the richest measure of the divine Presence, and become a body wholly filled and flooded with God Himself]!" (AMPC)*

As His child, the eyes of your understanding must be enlightened to His love for you. Seek His love. Understand by the Holy Spirit how intense His love is for all of His children.

~Prayer~

Dear Lord, please expand my capacity to receive Your love. Reveal to me more about how Your love was poured out on the cross. You are love, and You have poured Yourself into me by the Holy Spirit. Thank You now. In Jesus' name.

ALL GOOD

God's love is clearly unconditional in that He expresses His love toward its objects—you and me, i.e., His people—despite our disposition toward Him. In other words, God loves because it is His nature to love. 1 John 4:8 sets forth the truth:

> *"The one who does not love has not known God, because God is love." (NTE)*

The love that is God moves Him to "benevolent action." The word omnibenevolent describes God. It comes from the Latin word omni meaning all and meaning good or charitable. When it's said that God is omnibenevolent, the meaning is that God is absolutely good and that no action or motive or thought or feeling or anything else about Him is less than purely good. He is "all good."

The Bible provides many, many testimonies of God's goodness. The Gospel message is basically a true story of divine rescue. All people need God to rescue them. As Jesus said of His act of dying to redeem men, "No one has greater love than this: that he lay down his life for his friends." (John 15:13 TLV) Scripture makes clear the unconditional nature of God's love in two more passages. "For God loved the world so much that he gave his only Son so that anyone who believes in him shall not perish but have eternal life. God did not send his Son into the world to condemn it, but to save it." (John 3:16-17 TLB) 1 John 4:9–10 says,

> *"God showed how much he loved us by sending his only Son into this wicked world to bring to us eternal life through his death. In this act we see what real love is: it is not our love for God but his love for us when he sent his Son to satisfy God's anger against our sins." (TLB)*

~Prayer~

Lord, I want to know You and Your love, because You are wholehearted love. Thank You that Your love does not begin with me. It begins with You. So, today I decide in my heart to make Your love first in my life because Your love is first in You.

GOD'S LOVE INCLUDES ALL

Romans 2:11 reveals a love that includes all people:

> *"For God shows no partiality [undue favor or unfairness; with Him one man is not different from another]." (AMPC)*

God is not a respecter of persons. He does not treat some better than others based on their dress, level of income, the positions they hold, or who they know. He especially goes to great lengths for the hurting.

God's love can be defined as inclusive. It's a love that includes to make individual souls part of a whole. Mother Teresa said, "If you judge people, you have no time to love them."

~Prayer~

Father, I ask You to help me with hospitality toward others, especially those of the household of faith. Make me a lover of strangers—a lover of mankind. Help me exercise the love of God toward everyone. May I treat them with love like God treats them. In Jesus' name.

NOTHING CAN SEPARATE YOU

Meditate on Romans 8:35, 37–39

"Who shall ever separate us from Christ's love? Shall suffering and affliction and tribulation? Or calamity and distress? Or persecution or hunger or destitution or peril or sword? . . . Yet amid all these things we are more than conquerors and gain a surpassing victory through Him Who loved us. For I am persuaded beyond doubt (am sure) that neither death nor life, nor angels nor principalities, nor things impending and threatening nor things to come, nor powers, Nor height nor depth, nor anything else in all creation will be able to separate us from the love of God which is in Christ Jesus our Lord." (AMPC)

Verse 34 says

"Christ Jesus is the one who died—more than that, who was raised—who is at the right hand of God, who indeed is interceding for us." (ESV)

Christ is alive and is still actively loving you now. His love is not a memory. It has moment by moment actions by the omnipotent, risen Son of God aimed to bring you into everlasting joy.

~Prayer~

Thank You, Father, for Your Son Jesus. His love is my protection from separation. And nothing can separate me from His love. Omnipotent Jesus loves me with His might. He loves me moment by moment with no cut-off.

HANDPICKED

Ephesians 1:4 declares

> *"Even as [in His love] He chose us [actually picked us out for Himself as His own] in Christ before the foundation of the world, that we should be holy (consecrated and set apart for Him) and blameless in His sight, even above reproach, before Him in love."* (AMPC)

You are handpicked by God. He set you apart just for Himself. Even before you were born, He consecrated you to Himself. His heart is always aimed toward you. He wants all of you—all of your heart. You are loved. You are valuable and special. You are placed in Christ; your life is hidden in Christ. When you do make mistakes, He forgives you. You don't lose your God-given position of being sanctified. You remain blameless and above reproach because you are in Him. You are His redeemed.

~Prayer~

Lord, thank You for setting me apart. Thank You for handpicking me before the foundations of the earth were put in place. I am loved and valued by You. I am Yours, and You are mine.

FIRST LOVE

Together John 17:24 and John 15:9 define what first love looks like to the heart of the Godhead—in the Father, Son, and Holy Spirit. In John 17:24 Jesus says,

"Father, concerning that which You have given Me, I desire that they also may be with Me where I am, that they may behold My glory, which You have given Me, for You loved Me before the foundation of the world." (RcV) In John 15:9 the Lord says, "As the Father has loved Me, I also have loved you; abide in My love." (RcV) John 3:16 expresses God's love for all: "For God so loved the world that He gave His only begotten Son, that everyone who believes into Him would not perish, but would have eternal life." (RcV) God's love for you is so great. You came into salvation through LOVE! Jesus laid down His life for you. The way you came into salvation is the way salvation is sustained. Love calls for change and transition. Change is all about the external things God ordains. And transition is about the internal happenings.

You awaken to the truth of your placement in Christ. And Christ has a residency within you. This intimacy positions you in first love. The Holy Spirit draws you to fully embrace an identity as the beloved of God, a place where you live within the intimate affection that exists between the Father and the Son. This place in God awaits you. When you fully step into it and begin to live out of it, you see the glory of the Lord for yourself. You start to extend that glory to others through your life. You are the beloved of God because He has placed you in Him. His love for you has nothing to do with your performance. In Him you have what you need to demonstrate on earth what Heaven is really like. Think of these words or Heavenly realities: abundance, life without sickness, joy, peace, dominion, love, and so much more.

~Confession~

I step out of the place where I have accepted a measured amount of love. I step out of the place where I thought I had to perform to be loved. I step into first love. First love is the love the Father has for His Son. First love is the Father's intense love for Jesus now bestowed upon you. And Jesus is in you, and the Father is in Him. You love the Father and Son with first love in return.

AWAKENING TO GOD'S LOVE

John 15:9 is profound. In it Jesus says,

> "I have loved you, [just] as the Father has loved Me; abide in My love [continue in His love with Me]." (AMPC)

It is humanly impossible to wrap your mind all the way around the truth that the Father loves you just the same way He loves His Son Jesus. The Father loves adoring His Son so much that He wanted more children just like Him. God loves you with the same degree of love He has for Jesus. And get this, Jesus loves you with the same intense love, too. So you are "accepted in the Beloved"—loved. (See Ephesians 1:6.) When you awaken to the love of the Godhead for you, it's called first love. You are embraced by the love that exists between the Father and the Son. Accept and receive this love.

~Prayer~

Dear Father, open my eyes to see Your love. Forgive me for taking Your love for granted. I receive the love with which You love Your Son. Thank You for loving me just like You love Your beloved Son. I am accepted in the Beloved! In Jesus' name. Selah.

A GOOD PLAN

3 John 2 speaks of God prospering you:

> "Beloved, I pray that you may prosper in every way and [that your body] may keep well, even as [I know] your soul keeps well and prospers." (AMPC)

God had a good plan laid out for the lives of humans before they made an appearance on the earth. His plan was not a plan of failure, misery, poverty, sickness, disaster, or disease. His was a good plan for life, health, happiness, and fulfillment. And today, He always has a plan for healing and restoration. God is on your side. What you can't do for yourself, He will do for you. God will do His part, but you must do your part to believe and obey.

~Prayer~

Lord, I trust Your plan for my life. Even when I don't understand it, and things are hard, I will say, "God has a good plan for my life." When I want to give up, I'll say, "I trust Your plan." I will do my part. And I totally trust You to do Your part according to Your promises. In Jesus' name.

THE CREATION SPEAKS

Deuteronomy 11:18–19, 21 speaks of Heaven on earth

> "Therefore shall ye lay up these my words in your heart and in your soul, and bind them for a sign upon your hand, that they may be as frontlets between your eyes. And ye shall teach them your children, speaking of them when thou sittest in thine house, and when thou walkest by the way, when thou liest down, and when thou risest up. . . . That your days may be

> *multiplied, and the days of your children, in the land which the Lord sware unto your fathers to give them, as the days of heaven upon the earth." (KJV)*

You can have days of Heaven upon earth now! 1 Timothy 6:17 says He is, "the living God, who gives us richly all things to enjoy." (NKJV) Psalm 19 declares that the earthly creation speaks constantly about the power and character of God. Creation tells you day and night that He loves you and wants to richly bless you. Take in verses 1–4,

> *"The heavens declare the glory of God; and the firmament shows His handiwork. Day unto day utters speech, and night unto night reveals knowledge. There is no speech nor language where their voice is not heard. Their line has gone out through all the earth, and their words to the end of the world." (NKJV)*

And on the earth you can know Psalm 115:14, no matter what the enemy is doing. "May the Lord give you increase more and more, you and your children." (AMPC) Every day as you learn to fellowship with the Lord, more of the good things He has for your life will come to you. You will experience days of Heaven on earth.

~Prayer~

Father, thank You for Your love and the fellowship I can know in the Holy Spirit. I lift my hands to You. I enjoy Your presence. I enjoy days of Heaven on the earth. My life and holy praise I give to You!

FORGIVENESS

1 John 2:1–2 tells of Jesus the Advocate.

> *"My little children, I write you these things so that you may not violate God's law and sin. But if anyone should sin, we have an Advocate (One*

> *Who will intercede for us) with the Father—[it is] Jesus Christ [the all] righteous [upright, just, Who conforms to the Father's will in every purpose, thought, and action]. And He [that same Jesus Himself] is the propitiation (the atoning sacrifice) for our sins, and not for ours alone but also for [the sins of] the whole world." (AMPC)*

You as a believer are God's little child. Selah. Think of that. Pause and think. When you miss the mark, Jesus prays for you. And you in turn can run to Him within your heart and confess your sins. You can freely admit anything to Jesus, the righteous one. He is faithful and just to forgive sins and cleanse from all unrighteousness.

So says 1 John 1:9

> *"If we [freely] admit that we have sinned and confess our sins, He is faithful and just (true to His own nature and promises) and will forgive our sins [dismiss our lawlessness] and [continuously] cleanse us from all unrighteousness [everything not in conformity to His will in purpose, thought, and action]." (AMPC)*

~Prayer~

Thank You, Lord, for Your love. I am Your child; You are my Father. Forgive me for anything I have done or thought that violated Your law of love. I receive Your forgiveness and Your love and Your cleansing from all unrighteousness. I desire to conform to Your will and purpose in all thought and action. In Jesus' name.

NO FEAR IN LOVE

1 John 4:18 declares

18 | LOVE'S AIM

> *"There is no fear in love [dread does not exist], but full-grown (complete, perfect) love turns fear out of doors and expels every trace of terror! For fear brings with it the thought of punishment, and [so] he who is afraid has not reached the full maturity of love [is not yet grown into love's complete perfection]." (AMPC)*

There is no fear in love. Dread does not exist the verse says. God's love when complete and perfect expels every trace of terror. Fear produces the thought of punishment. He who is afraid has not matured. Mature love is complete and perfect.

Love has a beginning and a point of completion. First, God loves you. By faith, you receive His love. You then grow to love yourself in a balanced way. You give love back to God. And that love you give back to God is His love.

1 John 4:19 says

> *"We love Him, because He first loved us."*

~PRAYER~

Dear God, help me not to be afraid of the future. Mature me in love—the perfect and complete love in Christ. Thank You for first loving me. Help me to love others like You love me. In Jesus' name.

THE FORCE OF LOVE

1 Corinthians 13:8 declares,

> *"Love never fails [never fades out or becomes obsolete or comes to an end]."*

Did you know that love is the greatest force on the earth today? As it flows from the Spirit within, love is a weapon of warfare against the enemy of your soul. It's a force to be harnessed. This creative force was beautifully released in the life of the Christ. Jesus on earth was an extension of the love that flows from the Father's heart to all mankind. How amazing is God's love for you. God is love, and He's expressed His love in the person of Jesus. Love is the greatest thing in life. God loves you. Receive His love today.

~Prayer~

Dear Lord, help me to see Your love. Open the ears of my heart to receive the greatest thing in my life. Thank You, that Your love is complete and unfailing; thank You that it endures forever. In Jesus' name.

LOVE NEVER FAILS

There is no failure with love 1 Corinthians 13:8 says. Even when you miss the mark, God's love for you never fails. And because love never fails, whatever you do for the Lord in love will never fail. Love never fades out or loses its brightness. Love never loses its brilliance.

God's love for you will never disappear. His love will never come to an end. When you flow in God's love, you won't become obsolete. You will always be useful and never find yourself out of date. You are never too young or too old to function in the fruit of love.

~Prayer~

O Lord, thank You that Your love for me never fails. Help me to see with the eyes of my heart that Your love for me will never fade out. I'll never become obsolete in Your kingdom. Thank You that Your love for me is being revealed each and every day. In Jesus' name.

FOLLOW AFTER LOVE

1 Corinthians 14:1 says make love your aim—your great quest. Love, God's love, is like a treasure hidden for you to find. You must seek after this love; you must search for it. Do what it takes to discover love's meaning.

The verse also says,

> *"Eagerly pursue and seek to acquire [this] love." (AMPC)*

Love must be captured. Let it become an expedition to discover what God's love truly is in its fullness in Christ. Your greatest intention must be to gain love. The voice of God will lead you to His love because after all God is love. Love is who God is.

~Prayer~

Lord, help me to follow after You today. Help me to listen to Your voice of love. Let love become my greatest aim—my ultimate quest. Let love be the road I travel on my journey so as to find my purpose. In Jesus' name.

SECTION TWO

THE ENTRANCE OF HIS LOVE

Your heart functions as both the loving organ and the gateway of your being. You understand your makeup as you recall your salvation experience. When you heard the Gospel—the good news of how the Lord Jesus died on the cross for your sins, your heart was touched. You sensed the depth and the sweetness of His love for your soul, and you responded to His love. You couldn't help but love Him in return for all He did for you. Mark 12:30 commands:

> "And you shall love the Lord your God with all your heart, with all your soul, with all your mind, and with all your strength." (ESV)

And you respond with love because He first loved you 1 John 4:19 reveals. So you opened the door of your heart to believe in Him and received Him. You received Him into your spirit and were born again of the Spirit in your spirit, but it was your heart which first had to open up to let Him in. Psalm 119:130 says, "The entrance of Your words gives light; It gives understanding to the simple." (NKJV)

The section that follows ministers the entrance of His love through the Word. Let light and understanding come to you.

CALLED TO FRIENDSHIP WITH GOD

John 15:9–15 contains a call to friendship with God. It says

> *"I have loved you even as the Father has loved me. Live within my love. When you obey me you are living in my love, just as I obey my Father and live in his love. I have told you this so that you will be filled with my joy. Yes, your cup of joy will overflow! I demand that you love each other as much as I love you. And here is how to measure it—the greatest love is shown when a person lays down his life for his friends; and you are my friends if you obey me. I no longer call you slaves, for a master doesn't confide in his slaves; now you are my friends, proved by the fact that I have told you everything the Father told me." (TLB)*

Jesus loves you just as His Father loves Him. You must remain in and live on in His love. Jesus is calling you to continue growing in the Father's love as one who is "in Christ." Living in His love means obeying His Word just as He obeyed the Father's commandments and lived in the Father's love in the Gospels.

Jesus has shared His heart with you so that His joy and delight may be in you, and you can have full, complete, and overflowing joy and gladness. The greatest affection is shown by one who lays down His life for His friends. He no longer calls you a slave or servant; He calls you His friend for you know what He is doing. He confides in you.

~Prayer~

Thank You, Lord, for allowing me to live in Your love. I can now abide in joy to the full as I live in the Father's love. Help me to live in obedience to His Word so my life will overflow in His love.

THINK ABOUT HIS LOVE

1 John 4:16 is a verse about God's love

> *"And we know (understand, recognize, are conscious of, by observation and by experience) and believe (adhere to and put faith in and rely on) the love God cherishes for us. God is love, and he who dwells and continues in love dwells and continues in God, and God dwells and continues in him." (AMPC)*

Becoming aware of God's love for you is the great pursuit of a lifetime. This pursuit puts you on a wonderful journey that will satisfy you entirely and bless your life. Practice awareness of God's love. He loves you so very much. How do you gain awareness of God's love? Good question. Meditate on the Scriptures about love. Confess the promises of God aloud. Focus on His love. Think about His love all the time. Receive His love.

~Prayer~

God: You are love. And You love me! Help me to become more aware of Your love as I live my daily life. I receive revelation of Your love. I will let that love flow from my heart to the hearts of others. Thank You, Lord. I am becoming more and more aware of Your love. In Jesus' name. Amen.

LISTEN FOR HEAVEN'S SOUND

God says in Jeremiah 29:12–13,

> *"Then you will call upon Me, and you will come and pray to Me, and I will hear and heed you. Then you will seek Me, inquire for, and require Me [as a vital necessity] and find Me when you search for Me with all your heart." AMPC)*

God is always calling you, as God's child, unto Himself. He sounds the bells of Heaven so you will come into His presence. Some never hear because they are earthbound. He desires for His children, His sheep, to hear His voice. He wants you to hear the sound of the bells. He is your ever-present Shepherd. Walk in the stillness of His presence wherever you go.

~Prayer~

Dear Lord, I can call upon You at all times and pray. Your ears are always open to my voice. I am Your child; You recognize my voice. Help me to listen for the bells of Heaven. I desire to hear Your voice—the voice of my Shepherd. Help me to seek You with all of my heart. Thank You for Your presence. In Jesus' name I pray.

SEEK THE LORD

Psalm 105:4 instructs:

> "Seek, inquire of and for the Lord, and crave Him and His strength (His might and inflexibility to temptation); seek and require His face and His presence [continually] evermore." (AMPC)

Urgent times are here for believers. The need is to seek God's face and His presence like never before. What does it mean to seek something? Seek is a strong word that means crave, pursue, and go after what you desire. You must seek the Lord and His strength. You must put yourself under His protection. And seek to know the power of His grace. Everyone needs strength so look to the Mighty One for it. Seek His face forever. Seek, seek, and seek some more. Your seeking of God must never cease. The more you know of Him, the more you will want to know.

~Prayer~

Dear Heavenly Father, finding You more and more is the most important thing in my life. I need You more than anything. Continually, I will seek Your face. I will seek Your love and mercy. I will seek Your strength. I shall seek You all the while I live in this world. In Jesus' name.

TRUST HIM

Receive these words:

> *"Do not let your heart be troubled, nor let it be afraid. [Let My perfect peace calm you in every circumstance and give you courage and strength for every challenge.]" (John 14:27 AMPC)*

Take in John 14:1: "Trust in and rely on God; believe in and adhere to and trust in and rely also on Me." (AMPC) It's good to wait on Him. It strengthens dependence. Psalm 27:14 says "Wait and hope for and expect the Lord; be brave and of good courage and let your heart be stout and enduring. Yes, wait for and hope for and expect the Lord." (AMPC)

He's a secure anchor. So says Hebrews 6:16–20:

> *"Among men it is customary to swear by something greater than themselves. And if a statement is confirmed by an oath, that is the end of all quibbling. So in this matter, God, wishing to show beyond doubt that his plan was unchangeable, confirmed it with an oath. So that by two utterly immutable things, the word of God and the oath of God, who cannot lie, we who are refugees from this dying world might have a source of strength, and might grasp the hope that he holds out to us. This hope we hold as the utterly reliable anchor for our souls, fixed in the very certainty of God himself in Heaven, where Jesus has already entered on our behalf, having*

> *become, as we have seen, "High Priest for ever after the order of Melchizedek." (PHILLIPS)*

Keep speaking "I trust You." Wait for God to work with your eyes on Him. This posture gives evidence that you really do trust Him. Hope is something that is future-directed. Hope connects you to your inheritance in Heaven. Wait with expectation in hopeful trust. Keep your spiritual "antennae" out to pick up even the faintest glimmer of His presence.

~Prayer~

Lord, I love Your presence more than life itself. My thoughts turn toward You, and my heart's desire is to be with You. I trust You, Lord. "My times are in Your hands." (Psalm 31:15 NIV)

REFUGE

Psalm 62:5–8 says find refuge in the Lord.

> *"My soul, wait only upon God and silently submit to Him; for my hope and expectation are from Him. He only is my Rock and my Salvation; He is my Defense and my Fortress, I shall not be moved. With God rests my salvation and my glory; He is my Rock of unyielding strength and impenetrable hardness, and my refuge is in God! Trust in, lean on, rely on, and have confidence in Him at all times, you people; pour out your hearts before Him. God is a refuge for us (a fortress and a high tower). Selah [pause, and calmly think of that]!" (AMPC)*

As a member of God's family, you can trust in Him at all times—when things are good and when things are bad. The call is to live from faith to faith says Romans 1:17:

> *"For in the Gospel a righteousness which God ascribes is revealed, both springing from faith and leading to faith [disclosed through the way of faith that arouses to more faith]. As it is written, The man who through faith is just and upright shall live and shall live by faith." (AMPC)*

You develop character by trusting God in the difficult situations. The more your character becomes like Christ's, the more your ability in God is released. God knows He can trust you. You function as God intended you to function. So lean on, rely on, and have confidence in God no matter what you face in life. God is available as your high tower and fortress. Just pause a moment and think on that!

~Prayer~

Lord, forgive me for not fully trusting You. You are my strength and my refuge. You are my fortress. I stand within the high tower of Your presence. Thank You for being my help at all times. Selah.

SHELTER

John 15:7–8 reveals

> *"If you live in Me [abide vitally united to Me] and My words remain in you and continue to live in your hearts, ask whatever you will, and it shall be done for you. When you bear (produce) much fruit, My Father is honored and glorified, and you show and prove yourselves to be true followers of Mine." (AMPC)*

The shelter of God is not only a place to visit God, but it is also a place to dwell with Him. For those who do dwell with God, His presence becomes more than a refuge. It becomes a permanent address. When you abide in Christ even as He and the Father are one so you become one with

God. His life becomes your life. His virtue and His wisdom become yours. His spirit sustains you. You faint before Him; you become unable to resist Him. You find abandonment to Him, and in this surrender, you find perfect shelter.

~Prayer~

Lord, You are my shield and the horn of my salvation. I live because of You. You are my rock; You are my strength; You are my deliverer. You, Jesus, are my life-giver. I live because of You. Thank You for giving away Your life for me. Jesus—my Lord and Savior. Amen.

TUNE IN

God lives in your very body. He is closer to you than anyone.

1 Corinthians 6:19 asks

> *"Do you not know that your body is the temple (the very sanctuary) of the Holy Spirit Who lives within you, Whom you have received [as a Gift] from God?" (AMPC)*

It is possible to listen to God within you while you are listening to other people. You will need the help of His Spirit to respond to them appropriately. Ask Him to think through you. Ask Him to live through you. Ask Him to love through you. The Lord Jesus is alive in you through the person of the Holy Spirit. You are His temple—His home. You cannot respond well to others through your natural thought processes unaided by the Spirit. You'll only offer others dry crumbs when they need the bread of life. Be a channel of His love, joy, and peace by listening to Him as you listen to others and then speak His anointed words.

~Prayer~

Dear Lord, I belong to You. As I hear others speaking, I will listen to You. I will tune into You for the life-giving answers that flow from You to me. Then I'll channel joy, peace, and love to those I am listening to and talking to. Thank You for living in and through me. In Jesus' name. Selah.

NO FEAR

1 John 4:18 promises

> "There is no fear in love [dread does not exist], but full-grown (complete, perfect) love turns fear out of doors and expels every trace of terror! For fear brings with it the thought of punishment, and [so] he who is afraid has not reached the full maturity of love [is not yet grown into love's complete perfection]." (AMPC)

You are living in the last of the last days. The world system instills people with fear and dread. As God's child, you have the upper hand in the world. You respond to God with love because He first loved you.

1 John 4:19 states

> "We love Him, because He first loved us." "For God is love." (1 John 4:8)

And love flows from God. It's the fruit of the Holy Spirit says Galatians 5:22. God's love can shut the door to fear and dread in your life.

~Prayer~

Thank You, Lord, that there is no fear in love. Thank You that full-grown, complete, and perfect love turns fear out of doors. Thank You, Lord, for loving me even before I knew You. In Jesus' name.

THE DEEP CALLS

Psalm 42:1–2 expresses the cry:

> "As the hart pants and longs for the water brooks, so I pant and long for You, O God. My inner self thirsts for God, for the living God. When shall I come and behold the face of God?" (AMPC)

God pours out in verse 7,

> "[Roaring] deep calls to [roaring] deep at the thunder of Your waterspouts; all Your breakers and Your rolling waves have gone over me." (AMPC)

I'm reminded of the time in my life before I received the baptism of the Holy Spirit. It was hunger. When a person is hungry, the deepest part of His spirit begins to call out to God for what will fill that hunger. Just like I did not know what I hungered after, you might not know for what you cry. But God knows, and this cry touches the depths of His heart. It causes Him to respond.

You must desire to know Jesus with such an intensity that every other desire pales and fades away beside it. Only your desire to know Him remains in first place. Let the deep within begin to call out to the deep in God.

~Prayer~

Dear Lord, I want to know You. My heart longs to be in Your presence. To be with You is life—*zoe* life or the God-kind of life flowing to me as Your child. My heart calls to Your heart—deep to deep and heart to heart. I am Yours, and You are mine. In Jesus' name.

ETERNAL REALITIES

2 Corinthians 4:17–18 states

> *"For our light affliction, which is but for a moment, worketh for us a far more exceeding and eternal weight of glory; While we look not at the things which are seen, but at the things which are not seen: for the things which are seen are temporal; but the things which are not seen are eternal." (KJV)*

Always remember that the forces of darkness cannot conquer you as a child of God. In God's eyes, trouble is but for a moment, and it works out for you a more exceeding and eternal weight of glory. You are a child of faith. Do not look at the things that are seen, but instead look at the things that are unseen. The things not seen are more real than temporal things like troubles which come for a time. You can focus on eternal things that last forever.

~Prayer~

Thank You, Father, for what You have done. I have eternal life. I have the faith from You so I can overcome those things that try to overcome me. I walk in the supernatural power of my God. The enemy cannot win against me because I am an eternal being in Christ. In Jesus' name.

THE GIFT OF THE HOLY SPIRIT

In John 16:7–8, Jesus explains the gift of the Holy Spirit. He says,

> *"However, I am telling you nothing but the truth when I say it is profitable (good, expedient, advantageous) for you that I go away. Because if I do not go away, the Comforter (Counselor, Helper, Advocate, Intercessor, Strengthener, Standby) will not come to you [into close fellowship with*

> *you]; but if I go away, I will send Him to you [to be in close fellowship with you]. And when He comes, He will convict and convince the world and bring demonstration to it about sin and about righteousness (uprightness of heart and right standing with God) and about judgment." (AMPC)*

John 16:13 adds

> *"But when He, the Spirit of Truth (the Truth-giving Spirit) comes, He will guide you into all the Truth (the whole, full Truth). For He will not speak His own message [on His own authority]; but He will tell whatever He hears [from the Father; He will give the message that has been given to Him], and He will announce and declare you to the things that are to come [that will happen in the future]." (AMPC)*

~Prayer~

Lord, thank You for sending back to dwell in me Your very own Son by way of the Holy Spirit. The Spirit is my helper—the one who walks along beside me. He helps me. He strengthens me. He upholds me with His right hand. (See Psalm 63:8.) He enables me to overcome this world system. He fills me with the power to overcome. Amen. Selah. So be it.

AN OPEN HEART

> *"But we all, with unveiled face, beholding as in a mirror the glory of the Lord, are being transformed into the same image from glory to glory, just as from the Lord, the Spirit." (2 Corinthians 3:18 NASB)*

What is the meaning of being open or unveiled before God? Openness comes from unhindered and unreserved consecration. The Bible is the Word of God. It is a book full of God's light. And the light in it will only enlighten those who are open to its Author—God. To be enlightened by the glory of the Lord, you must behold Him with an unveiled face.

If you come to God with a veiled face, the glory will not enlighten you. If you are not open to God, you will not receive God's light. Many people carry closed hearts toward God. 2 Corinthians 4;4 explains

> *The god of this age has blinded the minds of unbelievers, so that they cannot see the light of the gospel that displays the glory of Christ, who is the image of God." (NIV)*

However, picture the case of a very small opening. If all the doors and windows of a room are closed, but just a crack is left open, light can still get in. It is not difficult for light to stream in. Open your heart at least a crack. Darkness results when you are closed. And being closed comes from a lack of consecration and a refusal to submit to God. Do you know that God is love? This truth will bring surrender.

Openness to God is not to be a temporary attitude. Instead, it's to become a permanent disposition you develop before God—a continuous practice. 2 Corinthians 13:16–17 reveals what happens when you turn to the Lord:

> *"But in the moment when one turns toward the Lord, the veil is removed. By 'the Lord' what I mean is the Spirit, and in any heart where the Spirit of the Lord is present, there is liberty." (VOICE)*

~Declaration of the Word~

> *"Now we see things imperfectly, like puzzling reflections in a mirror, but then we will see everything with perfect clarity. All that I know now is partial and incomplete, but then I will know everything completely, just as God now knows me completely." (1 Corinthians 13:12 NLT)*

DEAD TO SIN

Based on Romans 6, declare I am dead to sin. I no longer live in sin. Romans 6:2–4 reveals

> *"How can we who died to sin live in it any longer? Are you ignorant of the fact that all of us who have been baptized into Christ Jesus were baptized into His death? We were buried therefore with Him by the baptism into death, so that just as Christ was raised from the dead by the glorious [power] of the Father, so we too might [habitually] live and behave in newness of life." (AMPC)*

Declare verse 5:

> *"For if we have become one with Him by sharing a death like His, we shall also be [one with Him in sharing] His resurrection [by a new life lived for God]." (AMPC)*

Then state verses 7–11:

> *"For when a man dies, he is freed (loosed, delivered) from [the power of] sin [among men]. Now if we have died with Christ, we believe that we shall also live with Him, because we know that Christ (the Anointed One), being once raised from the dead, will never die again; death no longer has power over Him. For by the death He died, He died to sin [ending His relation to it] once for all; and the life that He lives, He is living to God [in unbroken fellowship with Him]. Even so consider yourselves also dead to sin and your relation to it broken, but alive to God [living in unbroken fellowship with Him] in Christ Jesus." (AMPC)*

You were raised to life with Him.

> *"For the law of the Spirit of life [which is] in Christ Jesus [the law of our new being] has freed me from the law of sin and of death."* (Romans 8:2 AMPC)

~Prayer~

O Lord, Father, thank You for sending Jesus to die on the cross in my place that I may have unbroken fellowship with You. My relationship to sin is broken because I died with You. I'm free. I am loosed. I am delivered from the spirit of sin and death. I've been raised into Christ's resurrection life. In Jesus' name.

CHRIST YOUR RIGHTEOUSNESS

Philippians 3:9 puts it well

> *"And that I may [actually] be found and known as in Him, not having any [self-achieved] righteousness that can be called my own, based on my obedience to the Law's demands (ritualistic uprightness and supposed right standing with God thus acquired), but possessing that [genuine righteousness] which comes through faith in Christ (the Anointed One), the [truly] right standing with God, which comes from God by [saving] faith."* (AMPC)

The one thing to desire is to be found and known in Christ. Hold firmly this attitude. You will not manifest perfect behavior as God leaves you weaknesses so that You will constantly draw on His help. You can stand before God and say, "Well, here I am Lord. I do not have a perfect record, but I do believe in Jesus."

~Prayer~

Lord, my righteousness is in You alone. It's not in my ability to perform. So, here I am, weaknesses and all, to be used as a vessel in Your hands. Thank You that I am found and known in You! In Jesus' name.

SHALOM

Shalom is a Hebrew word. Shalom is prosperity or everything that goes into the making of man's highest good. It's an abundance of everything. Shalom is translated as peace. Shalom inside you is directly related to shalom in your life outside of you. It comes from communion with Him.

I'm sensing as I write, "Come on into the secret place. Come right next to His heart. He has prepared a place beyond the veil. The atmosphere of Heaven is touching me right now. Fresh oil is flowing from Heaven. I step in to receive from Heaven. Everything I need is here in His presence. Shalom is flowing to me! God's healing oil—liquid love—overshadows me at this moment. Breath of Heaven, breathe on me now. Shine down, Lord. Show Your glory. Reveal Your face." You can pray this way, also.

~Prayer~

Dear Lord, there is no other place I would rather be than in Your presence. I'm one with You. Carry me into the Holy of Holies. Take me beyond the veil. I want to see Your face. I want to behold Your glory. In Jesus' name. So be it.

HE BEQUEATHS PEACE

The Word says depend on God and be free of distress. John 14:1 says rely on Jesus.

> *"Do not let your hearts be troubled (distressed, agitated). You believe in and adhere to and trust in and rely on God; believe in and adhere to and trust in and rely also on Me." (AMPC)*

Jesus promises in John 14:27,

> *"Peace I leave with you; My [own] peace I now give and bequeath to you. Not as the world gives do I give to you. Do not let your hearts be troubled, neither let them be afraid. [Stop allowing yourselves to be agitated and disturbed; and do not permit yourselves to be fearful and intimidated and cowardly and unsettled.]" (AMPC)*

And in John 14:16 is the promise of the Comforter forever:

> *"And I will ask the Father, and He will give you another Comforter (Counselor, Helper, Intercessor, Advocate, Strengthener, and Standby), that He may remain with you forever." (AMPC)*

~Prayer~

Thank You for going away and sending back the Holy Spirit—the Spirit of Truth—to live in me. (See John 16:13.) Jesus, by the Spirit You are with me and in me. You are my peace. You are the perfect Leader, and I will follow You. The Holy Spirit leads into all truth. (See Hebrews 2:10 and John 14:17.) I receive all the Father has for me through You, Jesus, as You and the Father are one. The Holy Spirit reveals Jesus so I am one with the Father, Son, and Holy Spirit. Thank You for preparing a place for me in Your presence and on the earth. In Jesus' name. So be it.

> *"You will show me the path of life; in Your presence is fullness of joy, at Your right hand there are pleasures forevermore." (Psalm 16:11 AMPC)*

THE STRAIGHT PATH

1 Thessalonians 5:17 says

> *"Pray continually." (NIV)*

God is calling His children to a life of constant communion with Him. Proverbs 3:6 instructs,

> *"In all your ways submit to him, and he will make your paths straight." (NIV)*

Everyone yearns for a simplified lifestyle. The call is to live above your circumstances even while involved in all the clutter that's part of life in this world. There is a place in Him where you can find rest. His presence awaits you always; He welcomes you as a beloved child. In that place of rest in God, He makes your paths straight.

~Prayer~

Lord, I answer the call to come into Your presence at any time. I acknowledge You even when life is cluttered and overwhelming. I come to You, and let You make my paths straight. Thank You for Your ways are good. In Jesus' name.

CHRIST MADE WISDOM

Psalm 119:130 declares

> *"The unfolding of your words gives light; it gives understanding to the simple." (NIV)*

There are none so full of knowing that God can't blind them with a hardened heart. And there are none so blind and ignorant that God can't open their mind and heart to the Gospel. The term "simple" in verse 130 is used in a good sense. It refers to the sincere and plain-hearted. Psalm 116:6 confirms God's heart for the simple. "The Lord preserves the simple; I was brought low, and He saved me." (NASB)

1 Corinthians 3:18 says of the worldly wise: "Let no one deceive himself. If anyone among you seems to be wise in this age, let him become a fool that he may become wise." (NKJV) To become a fool means here to forsake the wisdom of philosophy and receive the simple word concerning Christ and His cross. Consider the verses 1 Corinthians 3:21–23,

> *"So let no one boast of men. Everything belongs to you! Paul, Apollos or Cephas; the world, life, death, the present or the future, everything is yours! For you belong to Christ, and Christ belongs to God!" (PHILLIPS)*

And note Galatians 6:14, "Yet God forbid that I should boast about anything or anybody except the cross of our Lord Jesus Christ." (PHILLIPS)

To become wise is to say yes to the wisdom of God and make Christ everything to you. 1 Corinthians 1:30–31 says,

> *"Yet from this same God you have received your standing in Jesus Christ, and he has become for us the true wisdom, a matter, in practice, of being made righteous and holy, in fact, of being redeemed. And this makes us see the truth of scripture: 'He who glories, let him glory in the Lord.'" (PHILLIPS)*

It is God who makes Christ wisdom to you.

~Declaration~

It is of God that I participate in such a complete and perfect salvation—a salvation which makes my entire being (spirit, soul, and body) one with Christ and Christ everything to me. This work is altogether of God that I may boast and glory in Him and not in myself.

LOVE OPENS UP WISDOM

Proverbs 1:1–4 teaches you that wisdom is full of prudence. The passage reads,

> *"The proverbs (truths obscurely expressed, maxims, and parables) of Solomon son of David, king of Israel: That people may know skillful and godly wisdom and instruction, discern and comprehend the words of understanding and insight, receive instruction in wise dealing and the discipline of wise thoughtfulness, righteousness, justice, and integrity, that prudence may be given to the simple, and knowledge, discretion, and discernment to the youth." (AMPC)*

Prudence means good management. Prudent people do not operate in extremes. They are balanced and conduct themselves wisely. Verses to consider:

> *"My son, if sinners entice you, do not consent." (Proverbs 1:10 AMPC)*

> *"Blessed (happy, fortunate, prosperous, and enviable) is the man who walks and lives not in the counsel of the ungodly [following their advice, their plans and purposes], nor stands [submissive and inactive] in the path where sinners walk, nor sits down [to relax and rest] where the scornful [and the mockers] gather." (Psalm 1:1 AMPC)*

> *"Take no part in and have no fellowship with the fruitless deeds and enterprises of darkness, but instead [let your lives be so in contrast as to] expose and reprove and convict them." (Ephesians 5:11 AMPC)*
>
> *"If you will turn (repent) and give heed to my reproof, behold, I [Wisdom] will pour out my spirit upon you, I will make my words known to you." (Proverbs 1:23 AMPC)*

God is saying He will make His words known if you will listen to Him and repent when He corrects you. He will open up wisdom, and you will have more revelation than you could ever imagine.

In Christ, you can experience Isaiah 11:2: "And the Spirit of the Lord shall rest upon Him—the Spirit of wisdom and understanding, the Spirit of counsel and might, the Spirit of knowledge and of the reverential and obedient fear of the Lord." (AMPC)

Pray often Ephesians 1:17–20:

> *"[For I always pray to] the God of our Lord Jesus Christ, the Father of glory, that He may grant you a spirit of wisdom and revelation [of insight into mysteries and secrets] in the [deep and intimate] knowledge of Him, By having the eyes of your heart flooded with light, so that you can know and understand the hope to which He has called you, and how rich is His glorious inheritance in the saints (His set-apart ones), And [so that you can know and understand] what is the immeasurable and unlimited and surpassing greatness of His power in and for us who believe, as demonstrated in the working of His mighty strength, Which He exerted in Christ when He raised Him from the dead and seated Him at His [own] right hand in the heavenly [places]." (AMPC)*

LOVE OPENS UP WISDOM (2)

All you need to do is obey and do what God has told you to do. As you obey, the Holy Spirit opens up the Word. The Body has not even scratched the surface of the revelation that is in the Word of God. If you'll obey, He'll make His will clearly known. He will speak living words to you. He will speak personal words—rhema words.

~Admonitions~

> "Because they hated knowledge and did not choose the reverent and worshipful fear of the Lord, would accept none of my counsel, and despised all my reproof, Therefore shall they eat of the fruit of their own way and be satiated with their own devices." (Proverbs 1:29-31 AMPC)
>
> "The reverent fear and worshipful awe of the Lord [includes] the hatred of evil; pride, arrogance, the evil way, and perverted and twisted speech I hate. I have counsel and sound knowledge, I have understanding, I have might and power." (Proverbs 8:13-14 AMPC)
>
> "But whoso hearkens to me [Wisdom] shall dwell securely and in confident trust and shall be quiet, without fear or dread of evil." (Proverbs 1:33 AMPC)

~Prayer~

Lord, I pray for your help. I desire to be prudent in every situation. Thank You, Lord. Reveal to me hidden treasures within Your Word. Dear Lord, I hearken to You, the spirit of Wisdom. I shall dwell securely and in confident trust. I shall be quiet and live without fear or dread of evil. In Jesus' name.

HOW TO GET WISDOM

Proverbs 4:1–7 speaks of getting wisdom.

> *"Hear, my sons, the instruction of a father, and pay attention in order to gain and to know intelligent discernment, comprehension, and interpretation [of spiritual matters]. For I give you good doctrine [what is to be received]; do not forsake my teaching. When I [Solomon] was a son with my father [David], tender and the only son in the sight of my mother [Bathsheba], He taught me and said to me, Let your heart hold fast my words; keep my commandments and live. Get skillful and godly Wisdom, get understanding (discernment, comprehension, and interpretation); do not forget and do not turn back from the words of my mouth. Forsake not [Wisdom], and she will keep, defend, and protect you; love her, and she will guard you. The beginning of Wisdom is: get Wisdom (skillful and godly Wisdom)! [For skillful and godly Wisdom is the principal thing.] And with all you have gotten, get understanding (discernment, comprehension, and interpretation)." (AMPC)*

1 Chronicles 28:9 tells how to get wisdom.

> *"And you, Solomon my son, know the God of your father [have personal knowledge of Him, be acquainted with, and understand Him; appreciate, heed, and cherish Him] and serve Him with a blameless heart and a willing mind. For the Lord searches all hearts and minds and understands all the wanderings of the thoughts. If you seek Him [inquiring for and of Him and requiring Him as your first and vital necessity] you will find Him; but if you forsake Him, He will cast you off forever!" (AMPC)*

Don't forget His Word. Do not turn back from the words of His mouth. Do not forsake Wisdom. Ask for wisdom according to James 1:5–6: "If you want to know what God wants you to do, ask him, and he will gladly tell you, for he is always ready to give a bountiful supply of wisdom to all who ask him; he will not resent it. But when you ask him, be sure that you really expect him to tell you." (TLB)

Wisdom helps you make choices now that you will be happy with and unashamed over later.

~Prayer~

Dear Lord, I ask for wisdom—skillful and Godly wisdom. Help me to apply Your wisdom in my life. Thank You. In Jesus' name.

WHOLENESS

3 John 2 is a prayer for wholeness:

> "Beloved, I pray that you may prosper in every way and [that your body] may keep well, even as [I know] your soul keeps well and prospers." (AMPC)

Wholeness is the opposite of brokenness. How can God work to restore, renew, and remake you according to Psalm 23:5 in such a time of brokenness all around? Psalm 23:3 promises "He restores my soul." (NKJV) Psalm 23:5 says,

> "You prepare a table before me in the presence of my enemies. You anoint my head with oil; my [brimming] cup runs over." (AMPC)

Trust God in this process of bringing you to a new realm of spiritual empowerment. It takes wholeness to be successful. And wholeness is the fruit of God's grace working in you. Faith in God allows you to live and work in a world filled with seemingly insurmountable obstacles, uncertainties, and confusing aspects of life.

~Prayer~

Lord, I choose to trust You in all areas of my life. I let Your grace work in my life. I choose to walk in wholeness. In Jesus' name.

HOLDING HIS HAND

As I sat in the presence of my King Jesus and my Abba Father, I held onto Him. As I was before Him, the weight of His glory came. I basked in His loving arms. I didn't want to leave. The challenges I felt from life fell off of me. I prayed, "Lord, You are leading me step by step through this life. I hold Your hand in trusting dependence. When my future looks uncertain and feels flimsy, I trust You. Forgive me for those times when I have tried to figure life out on my own. I can do nothing apart from You, as John 15:5 confirms." The verse reads

> "I am the Vine; you are the branches. Whoever lives in Me and I in him bears much (abundant) fruit. However, apart from Me [cut off from vital union with Me] you can do nothing." (AMPC)

You can pray the same. You can encounter Him, too. Regarding the future Deuteronomy 29:29 discloses "The secret things belong unto the Lord our God, but the things which are revealed belong to us and to our children forever, that we may do all of the words of this law." (AMPC)

God promises in Psalm 32:8, "I [the Lord] will instruct you and teach you in the way you should go; I will counsel you with My eye upon you." (AMPC)

Genesis 28:15 says

> "And behold, I am with you and will keep (watch over you with care, take notice of) you wherever you may go." (AMPC)

~Prayer~

Thank You for showing me the next step forward and the one after that then the one after that. So, Lord, I choose to relax and enjoy the journey in Your presence. I trust You to open up the way for me as I go. In Jesus' name I pray.

DIRECTION

In John 14:6, Jesus reveals

> *"I am the Way and the Truth and the Life; no one comes to the Father except by (through) Me." (AMPC)*

Have you ever gotten lost while driving your car and found yourself refusing to stop and ask for directions? At times in your journey through life, you find you want to go your own way and do your own thing. As a result, you face great difficulty and hardship. You search and search for truth in different places but there remains only one way to God, and it's through Jesus Christ.

Declare, *I will follow Jesus because He IS the way, the truth, and the life. He leads me into all truth. He is the fullness of life.*

~Prayer~

Lord, thank You for Your Son, Jesus. You knew I needed help. I can walk in truth and abundant life because I follow the Lord. He is my way. I pray for those searching for truth in different places. God, open their eyes to see that Jesus is the only way to You, Father. And reveal Jesus as the only way to fullness of life. In His name I pray. Jesus said in John 10:10:

> *"My purpose is to give life in all its fullness." (TLB)*

TREASURE GOD'S WORD

Receive God's Word as treasure. Proverbs 7:1–4 encourages,

> *"My son, keep my words; lay up within you my commandments [for use when needed] and treasure them. Keep my commandments and live, and keep my law and teaching as the apple (the pupil) of your eye. Bind them on your fingers; write them on the tablet of your heart. Say to skillful and godly Wisdom, You are my sister, and regard understanding or insight as your intimate friend."*

God has created you to be dependent on Him. John 15:5 states,

> *"I (the Lord) am the vine; you are the branches. If you remain in me and I in you, then you will produce much fruit. Without me, you can't do anything." (CEB)*

You must bring Him your challenges and allow Him to help you. Only God knows what is in your heart, and He is the expert at removing the worthless things while retaining what's valuable. (See Malachi 3:3.)

~Prayer~

Father, help me to stay on course. Deliver me from any and all distractions that would block me from putting Your Word and Your commandments in first place in my life. Grant me a fresh hunger for Your Word. I take this hunger for truth now. I receive it now. My faith in the Word is a now faith. In Jesus' name.

GOD IS PLEASED

Proverbs 4:8–9 instructs

> *"Prize Wisdom highly and exalt her, and she will exalt and promote you; she will bring you to honor when you embrace her. She shall give to your head a wreath of gracefulness; a crown of beauty and glory will she deliver to you." (AMPC)*

Verse 12 of the same chapter reveals more about what happens when you "prize wisdom." God will bless your walk with Him. "When you walk, your steps shall not be hampered [your path will be clear and open]; and when you run, you shall not stumble." (AMPC)

Verse 18 reveals the fullness of the walk in wisdom: "But the path of the [uncompromisingly] just and righteous is like the light of dawn, that shines more and more (brighter and clearer) until [it reaches its full strength and glory in] the perfect day [to be prepared]." (AMPC)

Look at 2 Samuel 23:4 for a picture of God's shining: "He dawns on them like the morning light when the sun rises on a cloudless morning, when the tender grass springs out of the earth through clear shining after rain." (AMPC)

You will fulfill Matthew 5:14: "You are the light of the world. A city set on a hill cannot be hidden." (AMPC)

And you will become a star. Philippians 2:15 says:

> *"That you may show yourselves to be blameless and guileless, innocent and uncontaminated, children of God without blemish (faultless, unrebukable) in the midst of a crooked and wicked generation [spiritually perverted and perverse], among whom you are seen as bright lights (stars or beacons shining out clearly) in the [dark] world." (AMPC)*

God is not angry with you because you have not yet arrived. He is pleased with you because you "press on toward the goal for the prize of the upward call of God in Christ Jesus." (Philippians 3:13 NASB) Keep walking the walk. A walk involves taking one step at a time. And God expects your spiritual growth to take some time. He is patient and will stay right with you until you reach your destination.

~Prayer~

Lord, thank You for the walk You've given me with You. I believe I am on time. My timing is not Your timing. I believe I will stay the course. I will complete the course. In You, I have strength for the journey. I now walk with You. Thank You. In Jesus' name.

GOD'S REST AND REFRESHMENT

Sit quietly in His presence and hear the Spirit say

"Come to Me, all you who labor and are heavy-laden and overburdened, and I will cause you to rest. [I will ease and relieve and refresh your souls.] Take My yoke upon you and learn of Me, for I am gentle (meek) and humble (lowly) in heart, and you will find rest (relief and ease and refreshment and recreation and blessed quiet) for your souls. For My yoke is wholesome (useful good—not harsh, hard, sharp, or pressing, but comfortable, gracious, and pleasant), and My burden is light and easy to be borne." (Matthew 11:28–30 AMPC)

His yoke is easy. His burdens are light. The Spirit says, *Take! Take! Take My light—My life-giving force. Take Me. Take Who I am: Life for the living and life-giving love.* You are empowered to go to the place of pure light in God. You are empowered to go to the place of pure love.

"God is light, and in him is no darkness at all." (1 John 1:5 ESV)

> "God is love." (1 John 4:8 ESV)

So come away with Me, the Lord says. Stay on the path with Me. Stick with Me. Remain in Me and rest.

~Prayer~

Wash me. Cleanse me so I can walk in places of light and love in God.

YOUR FAMILY

It's a season to pour into your family. What do you pour into them? God's love!

Note Psalm 92:15: "To shew that the Lord is upright: he is my rock, and there is no unrighteousness in him." (KJV) Demonstrate it. Speak over them the promise of verses 12–15

> "The [uncompromisingly] righteous shall flourish like the palm tree [be long-lived, stately, upright, useful, and fruitful]; they shall grow like a cedar in Lebanon [majestic, stable, durable, and incorruptible]. Planted in the house of the Lord, they shall flourish in the courts of our God. [Growing in grace] they shall still bring forth fruit in old age; they shall be full of sap [of spiritual vitality] and [rich in the] verdure [of trust, love, and contentment]. [They are living memorials] to show that the Lord is upright and faithful to His promises; He is my Rock, and there is no unrighteousness in Him." (AMPC)

Romans 9:14 also speaks of the perfect God. "What shall we say then? Is there unrighteousness with God? God forbid." (KJV)

~Prayer~

Thank You, Father, for this season of life. Thank You for my family. You chose them for me before the foundations of the earth. Help me, Father, to be a living memorial before them of Your goodness and perfect righteousness. Thank You for loving my family through me. My life is in Your hands. "My times are in your hands" (Psalm 31:15 NIV) These things I pray. In Jesus' name. Amen.

LET THE LORD BE THE BUILDER

Verse 1 from Psalm 127 teaches:

> *"Except the Lord builds the house, they labor in vain who build it; except the Lord keeps the city, the watchman wakes but in vain." (AMPC)*

No matter what you build, the Lord must be the builder or your work will be in vain. You may be building a family, a ministry, or a career, or your life as a whole, but if the Lord is not involved in it, the results will not last in the test. The Lord must be your senior partner in life. When He is senior, you find you enter into His rest. He wants to be a part of everything you do. Let Him be your builder. Your life will not be lived in vain.

~Prayer~

Lord, without You I cannot do anything. You are my partner in life. Everything that I am or that I do in this life, I ask You to be a part of it. Forgive me, if and when I have tried to do life on my own. I fail on my own. I need You to be my builder. Then because of You whatever I do, it will not be in vain. Amen.

PRAISE

Psalm 145:1–2 says,

> *"I will extol You, my God, O King; and I will bless Your name forever and ever [with grateful, affectionate praise]. Every day [with its new reasons] will I bless You [affectionately and gratefully praise You]; yes, I will praise Your name forever and ever."* (AMPC)

God is good! Each day brings the opportunity to lift your hands and heart to God in affectionate praise with gratitude for who He is and who you are to Him. Each day brings brand new reasons to praise and worship Him all the time.

~Prayer~

Lord, each day I will praise You for Your goodness. I will bless Your name while I live. I will shout praises to You while I have breath. I will extol You, my King and my God. You are my God who is good all the time. Thank You for being so good to me, Your servant. Thank You for Your unfailing love. In Jesus' name.

SECTION THREE

LOVE SEARCHES THE HEART

There are times when you do not know your own heart. You think you are willing to obey, and you think you really desire the will of God, but you do not realize that in the deepest part of your heart lies hidden motives and a stubborn, unyielded self-will. Therefore, you must cry as David cried before God, "Examine me, O Lord, and try me; test my inward parts and my heart." (Psalms 26:2)

You should pray daily,

> "Search me, O God, and know my heart: try me, and know my thoughts: and see if there be any wicked way in me, and lead me in the way everlasting." (Psalms 139:23–24)

Only when God searches you and knows your heart before Him will you know your heart rightly. Let the passages in this section do a thorough work of searching.

SEARCH ME AND KNOW ME

No detail of your life is hidden from your Lord. He sees that everything you need is here; it's in the presence of the Lord. Life flows to you from Heaven. Let Psalm 139:1-4 be your prayer

> "O Lord, you have searched me and known me! You know when I sit down and when I rise up; you discern my thoughts from afar. You search out my path and my lying down and are acquainted with all my ways. Even before a word is on my tongue, behold, O Lord, you know it altogether." (ESV)

Allow the light of His healing presence to shine into the deepest recesses of your being. Let His Spirit cleanse, heal, refresh, and renew you.

Acknowledge that everything you need cost Him His life. Forgiveness is at the very core of His abiding presence. Hebrews 13:5 records, "For he has said, 'I will never leave you nor forsake you.'"

~Prayer~

Father, no one understands me or knows me like You do. No one knows me or loves me like You do. Fill me with Your love. Make me a reservoir of love that flows over into the lives of the people around me.

ABIDING IN LOVE

To abide in His love, His mighty, saving, keeping, satisfying love, even as He (Jesus) abode in the Father's love—surely the very greatness of our calling teaches us that it never can be a work we have to perform; it must be with us as with Him, the result of the spontaneous outflowing of a life from within, and the mighty inworking of the love from above.

What we only need is this: to take time and study the divine image of this life of love set before us in Christ.

—From *Abide in Christ* by Andrew Murray

Love fulfills the law. Galatians 5:14–16 states how this is so.

> *"For the entire law is fulfilled in keeping this one command: 'Love your neighbor as yourself.' If you bite and devour each other, watch out or you will be destroyed by each other. So I say, walk by the Spirit, and you will not gratify the desires of the flesh." (NIV)*

If you love someone, you won't sin against him. Why would anyone choose another way? Many people have a low faith level and a high fear level. Often they lack knowledge of God's Word. When you abide in God's love, you find you can trust Him. God meets your need for love. Following Jesus Christ is the only way to find an abundant and secure life. He is your security; He gives security for all eternity.

~Prayer~

Lord, thank You for showing me Your salvation through Your Word, for Your Word is life—even marrow to my bones. Your Word is truth and strength. Thank You for meeting all my needs in Christ Jesus. I purpose in my heart to seek Your kingdom and righteousness first. In Jesus' matchless name. Amen.

DO YOU LOVE YOURSELF?

James 2:8 teaches,

> *"If indeed you [really] fulfill the royal Law in accordance with the Scripture, You shall love your neighbor as [you love] yourself, you do well." (AMPC)*

Do you love yourself? In order to fulfill the royal law, you must love yourself before you can love your neighbor. Ponder this in your heart. You must love yourself first to be capable of love for others. Then you will do well. You'll be successful in love.

Man's way is a way of selfish love—a love that is easily provoked, blames others, strikes out, and causes deep emotional pain. Man's way of selfish love results in failure and abandonment. God's way offers unconditional love that meets your deepest yearnings. He alone promises to "never leave or forsake you." And He keeps this promise. Ephesians 4:19 testifies, "And it is he who will supply all your needs from his riches in glory because of what Christ Jesus has done for us." (TLB)

Take to heart Hebrews 13:5 TLB, "Stay away from the love of money; be satisfied with what you have. For God has said, 'I will never, never fail you nor forsake you,'" and Matthew 6:31–32, TLB:

> *"So don't worry at all about having enough food, and clothing. Why be like the heathen? For they take pride in all these things and are deeply concerned about them. But your heavenly Father already knows perfectly well that you need them, and he will give them to you if you give him first place in your life and live as he wants you to."*

Seek first His kingdom and His righteousness.

~Prayer~

Lord, grace me to love myself like You love me. Help me receive true love from You so I can love You and love others as You love me. In Jesus' name I pray.

THE GREAT COMMANDMENTS

Matthew 22:36-39 records Jesus' answer about the commandments:

> "Teacher, which kind of commandment is great and important (the principal kind) in the Law? [Some commandments are light—which are heavy?] And He replied to him, You shall love the Lord your God with all your heart and with all your soul and with all your mind (intellect). This is the great (most important, principal) and first commandment. And a second is like it: You shall love your neighbor as [you do] yourself." (AMPC)

These commandments are things you must choose to do; you must decide for yourself to obey them. You alone must make a commitment to embrace them. Ask yourself, "Will I continue to be a part of the problem or be part of the answer?" Be part of the answer. Align your heart with the great commandments.

~Prayer~

Lord, I choose to be part of the answer and not part of the problem. I choose love. Love for You and my neighbors will be the central theme of my life today and always. In Jesus' name.

HOW IS YOUR LOVE WALK?

John 13:35 says your love walk marks you as a disciple. The verse reads,

> "By this shall all [men] know that you are My disciples, if you love one another [if you keep on showing love among yourselves]." (AMPC)

God's love in you noticed by the world is to cause the ungodly to see God. How is your love walk? Is it the main theme of your life? The world will only be impressed by a consistent love walk among Christians. Such walks are rarely seen and impossible to maintain without leaning upon Jesus Christ. When people see real love, they WILL see God. It's your behavior toward the other believers that shows love which can be seen by the world.

~Prayer~

Lord Jesus, thank You for Your love in me. Help me to be Jesus to all whom I meet and interact with in the world that they may see and know that I am Your disciple. May their lives be changed. May they desire in their hearts to want the same Jesus who has transformed me into a disciple. In the name of Jesus.

LOVE IS THE KEY

1 Corinthians 13:1–3 says of love,

> *"Though I speak with the tongues of men and of angels, but have not love, I have become sounding brass or a clanging cymbal. And though I have the gift of prophecy, and understand all mysteries and all knowledge, and though I have all faith, so that I could remove mountains, but have not love, I am nothing. And though I bestow all my goods to feed the poor, and though I give my body to be burned, but have not love, it profits me nothing." (AMPC)*

Love is the key that opens the door to everything you need. Love is the foundation; it's also the spiritual weapon. Love is the main thing. All of the gifts of the Spirit hang on love. If you don't have the God kind of love, you just make a big noise. Without love, you are a useless nobody. Even if you feed the poor and surrender your very life, you gain nothing when you do it with the wrong motive and the lack of love.

~Prayer~

Dear Lord, help me to walk in Your love. I am a person who operates in God's love. I refuse to be someone who makes a lot of noise and has no love. I am a useful vessel in the Lord's hands. Lord, I will allow Your love to flow through me especially to my family and loved ones. In Jesus' name. Selah.

NOTHING WITHOUT LOVE

1 Corinthian 13:2 says a follower of Christ is nothing without love:

> "If I speak God's Word with power, revealing all his mysteries and making everything plain as day, and if I have faith that says to a mountain, "Jump," and it jumps, but I don't love, I'm nothing." (MSG)

Nothing means nothing! It means you are a thing that does not exist. You are not anything. You are a zero.

~Prayer~

Dear Lord, I need You. Without You, I'm nothing. No matter what I do or accomplish in this life, if I do it without You, it will remain as nothing. I receive You into my life as Lord and Savior. I believe Jesus is the Son of God who died for me. Come into my heart and save me from being a nothing. I want to live a life that is alive in You and real. In Jesus' name. Amen.

VITAL CONNECTION

John 15:7 says,

> *"If you live in Me [abide vitally united to Me] and My words remain in you and continue to live in your hearts, ask whatever you will, and it shall be done for you."* (AMPC)

You must stay vitally united and connected to Jesus, Your Savior and Lord. Fruit cannot grow apart from the vine, tree, or plant to which it was meant to be attached. As a believer, the same is true for you. You must spend time in His presence to grow and bear fruit. Dwell with, abide, take up residence in Jesus. Allow Jesus to be the source for your life. Stay connected to Jesus. Then whatever you ask, in accordance with His Word, will be done for you.

~Prayer~

Holy Spirit, help me to stay vitally connected to Jesus. He is my life source. He is the true vine; I am the branch. I can do nothing without Him. Thank You, Lord, for Your life flowing through me. Amen.

JESUS: YOUR SYMPATHETIC HIGH PRIEST

Hebrews 4:15 reveals,

> *"For we do not have a High Priest Who is unable to understand and sympathize and have a shared feeling with our weaknesses and infirmities and liability to the assaults of temptation, but One Who has been tempted in every respect as we are, yet without sinning."* (AMPC)

When you have difficulty keeping your focus on the Lord, you can become discouraged. He is aware of your heart's desire to be in His presence continually. So don't let feelings of failure weigh you down. The world is rigged to distract you from His presence. However, He is with you. He'll never leave you. The Lord Jesus is your High Priest—your access to God. He understands and sympathizes with your feelings of weakness as He was tempted in every respect as you, yet He never sinned.

~Prayer~

Lord, thank You for sending Jesus as my High Priest and great intercessor. Help me to receive more revelation of Your intense love. I rest in the fact— the truth— that Your presence is always over my life. I know You will never leave me. In Jesus' name.

ARE YOU THIRSTY?

Are you thirsty like the deer mentioned in Psalm 42:1? The verse reads,

> *"As the deer pants for the water brooks, So my soul pants for You, O God."* (NASB)

The deer is very thirsty. When deer drink stream water, they stand calmly in one place and they bend down their heads to lap the water. Deer, overheated from running, pant with great thirst as they yearn for cool water. Have you ever experienced intense thirst? The sensation of thirst comes especially when you've expended a lot of energy in daily living. You long for a drink.

Revelation 7:16 promises,

> *"They shall hunger no more, neither thirst any more."* (AMPC)

The passage speaks of the state of continual perfect spiritual health and satisfaction that exists in Heaven in the presence of the Savior.

~Prayer~

Lord, You are the Living Water. I come to You now and drink. You promised that I won't hunger or thirst anymore. So now I receive fresh, living water flowing from You to my soul. In Jesus' name.

GUARD YOUR HEART AGGRESSIVELY

Ephesians 3:20 says of God:

> "Now to Him Who, by (in consequence of) the [action of His] power that is at work within us, is able to [carry out His purpose and] do superabundantly, far over and above all that we [dare] ask or think [infinitely beyond our highest prayers, desires, thoughts, hopes, or dreams]." (AMPC)

Do you ever find yourself saying something that contradicts what you've prayed? If so, there is a heart issue that needs attention as your words spoken aloud should match the words you pray to the Father.

Your heart affects your soul and body. And your soul includes your mind, will, and emotions. This interrelationship is why it is so important to guard what you see and hear for those things affect the heart. When your heart is right, so, too, is your life. Whatever your heart holds to as its standard becomes a fixture in your mind. When the Father has your whole heart, He responds to the things you pray for from your heart with a "yes and amen" every time. The Bible instructs, "I have stored up your word in my heart, that I might not sin against you." (Psalm 119:11 ESV) When you pray according to the Word stored inside, God brings those prayers to pass as He is a God of blessing.

Proverbs 4:23 instructs, "Keep and guard your heart with all vigilance and above all that you guard, for out of it flow the springs of life." (AMPC) Many people are deceived into believing they cannot help what they think. But the truth is you can choose your thoughts. You must think about what you have been thinking about. When you do so, it doesn't take very long to discover the root cause of your attitude. The enemy of your soul will try to fill your mind with wrong thinking, but you do not have to receive anything he tries to put in you.

Guard your heart aggressively. Let your thoughts be good thoughts. Think about things that are honorable and true. Let Philippians 4:8 prevail:

"Fix your thoughts on what is true and good and right. Think about things that are pure and lovely, and dwell on the fine, good things in others. Think about all you can praise God for and be glad about." (TLB)

~Prayer~

Father, I choose to do the honorable thing so then Your honor will hold me up. I submit and commit to doing what You say in Your Word. I have utmost respect for Your Word and Your ways. I put aside feelings and human reasoning and simply obey! In Jesus' name. Amen.

FACE THE TRUTH

Psalm 51:6 says of God,

> "Behold, You desire truth in the inner being; make me therefore to know wisdom in my inmost heart."

Truth is the person of Jesus John 14:6 states. The Holy Spirit is the Spirit of Truth says John 16:13. You and I must be hid in God. Light and darkness cannot merge.

In Psalm 51, David cries to God for mercy and forgiveness after the Lord has dealt with him about his sin with Bathsheba and murder of Uriah. David had committed these sinful acts about one full year before He wrote Psalm 51. David did not acknowledge his sin until long after the act. He wasn't willing to face the truth. Sometimes, you are not willing to face the truth about things you've done or things done to you. Because God desires truth in the inner being, repentance is in order so you can receive God's forgiveness and go on to walk again under blessing.

~Prayer~

Lord, thank You for a way out when I say or do things that miss the mark. I choose to face the truth and repent quickly. I choose to receive Your forgiveness and walk under the blessings of obedience. Amen.

THE SPIRIT'S RULE

The Lord says in Proverbs 4:20

> *"My son, attend to my words; consent and submit to my sayings." (AMPC)*

Consent means to feel agreement in your heart. It means to approve and say "yes" to it. Submit means to yield to the Word and permit its rule over your soul. When you yield to the Word, you give it control and power over you; you give in to it. You consider it, or regard it; and take action on it.

Proverbs 4:21 says keep the Word in the center of your heart. In the Bible, heart refers to the soul: the mind, will, and emotions. The Word can positively impact your physical body:

> *"For they (God's words) are life to those who find them, healing and health to all their flesh." (Proverbs 4:22 AMPC)*

You are a tri-partite being made up of a spirit, a soul, and a body. Your spirit is joined to the Spirit of the Lord when you are born again. 1 Corinthians 6:17 says you are one spirit with the Lord. When the Spirit of God in union with your spirit rules your being, the life of God flows out to your soul. This life manifests the glory of God in your body. It's up to you to guard this flow. Verse 23 says,

> *"Keep and guard your heart with all vigilance and above all that you guard, for out of it flow the springs of life." (AMPC)*

~Prayer~

Lord, help me to guard my heart with great vigilance. Help me examine my thoughts and my attitudes on a regular basis and make adjustments to bring them in line with the Word as needed. Thank You. In Jesus' name.

THINK ABOUT YOUR THOUGHTS

Proverbs 4:23 calls for controlling your thoughts. "Keep and guard your heart with all vigilance and above all that you guard, for out of it flow the springs of life." (AMPC)

Many people are deceived into believing they cannot help what they think. The truth is you can choose your thoughts. Ask yourself, "what are you thinking about?" And think about what you have been thinking about. If you'll pay attention to your thoughts, you will be able to pin-point the root cause of a bad attitude. The enemy of your soul is always trying to fill your mind with wrong thinking. Don't eat His poison. Think on good things. Think on God's Word. Think on Jesus. Philippians 4:8 says,

> *"For the rest, brethren, whatever is true, whatever is worthy of reverence and is honorable and seemly, whatever is just, whatever is pure, whatever is*

> *lovely and lovable, whatever is kind and winsome and gracious, if there is any virtue and excellence, if there is anything worthy of praise, think on and weigh and take account of these things [fix your minds on them]."* (AMPC)

In considering your thoughts, consider where they are taking you. Proverbs 4:26–27 directs, "Consider well the path of your feet, and let all your ways be established and ordered aright. Turn not aside to the right hand or to the left; remove your foot from evil." (AMPC)

~Prayer~

Thank you, Lord, I choose to guard my heart well and let my thoughts be good thoughts. I will think on things that are honorable and true. I will watch my heart change as I capture thoughts and make them obey the Lord according to 2 Corinthians 10:5: "Casting down imaginations, and every high thing that exalteth itself against the knowledge of God, and bringing into captivity every thought to the obedience of Christ." (KJV)

EXAMINE YOUR COMMUNICATION

Proverbs 8:6–9 provides a standard:

> *"Hear, for I will speak excellent and princely things; and the opening of my lips shall be for right things. For my mouth shall utter truth, and wrongdoing is detestable and loathsome to my lips. All the words of my mouth are righteous (upright and in right standing with God); there is nothing contrary to truth or crooked in them. They are all plain to him who understands [and opens his heart], and right to those who find knowledge [and live by it]."* (AMPC)

James 3:10 gives great guidance.

> *"Out of the same mouth come forth blessing and cursing. These things, my brethren, ought not to be so." (AMPC)*

Listen to Proverbs 31:26, "She (the wise soul) opens her mouth in skillful and godly Wisdom, and on her tongue is the law of kindness [giving counsel and instruction]." (AMPC)

The fruit of wisdom in your speech is Proverbs 8:21:

> *"That I may cause those who love me to inherit [true] riches and that I may fill their treasuries."*

~Prayer~

God, may I be excellent in my speech. May I speak words that are righteous and true. Lord, help me to engage in plain, straightforward, honest, and truthful communication. Help me not to "talk in circles." Thus my memory will be a blessing according to Proverbs 10:7: "The memory of the [uncompromisingly] righteous is a blessing." (AMPC)

OVERCOME NEGATIVES WITH POSITIVE THANKSGIVING

Pay attention to the confession of Psalm 116:17:

> *"I will offer to You the sacrifice of thanksgiving and will call on the name of the Lord." (AMPC)*

To protect and preserve a heart of thankfulness, you must remember that you live in a fallen world where blessings and sorrows intermingle freely. The psalmist says he will call on the Lord, but only after he has offered up to God the sacrifice of thanksgiving. Sometimes people call upon the name of the Lord and their lives are filled with complaining and not thanks. There is absolutely no positive power in complaining; complaining releases only negative power. Thankfulness, by contrast, releases the very power of God in your life—a very positive power.

~Prayer~

Dear Lord, forgive me for not being thankful. I commit to praise You and thank You through the day. I call upon Your name in new freedom as I stay thankful no matter what is taking place. The light of Your presence is shining on me. Thank You for being my steadfast companion. In Jesus' name.

THE FATHER PRUNES

The Gospel of John continues in chapters 14, 15, and 16 with the last words of Jesus to His disciples. Jesus was preparing His followers for His departure. But He would return to them through the Holy Spirit—the Spirit who would lead them into all truth. (See John 16:13.) They would be able to know and see Jesus in the spirit. He would not be visible to the naked eye, but He would be more real to them than He had been in physical form. Jesus states in John 15:1-2,

> *"I am the True Vine, and My Father is the Vinedresser. Any branch in Me that does not bear fruit [that stops bearing] He cuts away (trims off, takes away); and He cleanses and repeatedly prunes every branch that continues to bear fruit, to make it bear more and richer and more excellent fruit."* (AMPC)

Believers are the branches. The Vinedresser, the Father, prunes you. He cuts away things so you'll not fail to produce the kind of fruit He desires. The cutting away is often painful. And sometimes you do not understand it. But the pruning is necessary for you to grow into the fruit-bearing branch of Jesus the Father wants you to be. The Father's work is progressive. And at times He needs to prune you to get you to higher places.

~Prayer~

Father, I desire to go higher. I desire to go to the highest place in You. Take away anything in me that does not belong there. Remove anything in me that You did not put there. Thank You for cleansing me. Thank You for making me clean through Your Word. In Jesus' name. John 15:3 says,

> "Now ye are clean through the word which I have spoken unto you." (KJV)

LEARNING TO RELEASE

The Word says,

> "And when you stand praying, if you hold anything against anyone, forgive them, so that your Father in heaven may forgive you your sins." (Mark 11:25 NIV)

Did you know that forgiveness is the heartbeat of Heaven? Once you are in Heaven, you will see those who have wronged you differently. You will be thankful that, while on earth, you freely made the right choice. You prayed, "Father forgive them. They don't know what they are doing." Jesus prayed this in Luke 23. Forgiveness is the foundation of what makes the Gospel "good news." You are forgiven by God.

In turn, learning to release offenses, wounds, and pain caused by others is extremely important. What is forgiveness exactly? To forgive is defined as to send away, to send forth, to yield up, to let go, to give up a debt, to remit. Forgiving is like untying a boat and letting it flow down the river.

Forgiving is not optional; it's mandatory. You can't remain in fellowship with God and hold onto unforgiveness.

Mark 11:23–25,

> *"Truly I tell you, if anyone says to this mountain, 'Go, throw yourself into the sea,' and does not doubt in their heart but believes that what they say will happen, it will be done for them. Therefore I tell you, whatever you ask for in prayer, believe that you have received it, and it will be yours. And when you stand praying, if you hold anything against anyone, forgive them, so that your Father in heaven may forgive you your sins." (NIV)*

~Prayer~

Lord, I am a believer. I have been forgiven a debt I cannot pay. A sin debt. I choose today to obey Your Word where it says,

> *"Above all, love each other deeply, because love covers over a multitude of sins." (1 Peter 4:8 NIV)*

Father, I remit every offense against me by (insert offender's name). I ask that the blood of Jesus cover these offenses. My love covers them. I ask that the sins be cast into the sea of forgetfulness, never again to be remembered. In Jesus' name. Amen. (See Micah 7:19 and Jeremiah 31:34.)

CLOTHE YOURSELVES

Colossians 3:12–13 reads,

> *"Therefore, as God's chosen people, holy and dearly loved, clothe yourselves with compassion, kindness, humility, gentleness and patience. Bear with each other and forgive one another if any of you has a grievance against someone. Forgive as the Lord forgave you." (NIV)*

Forgiving offenses against you is the ground for the release of God's forgiveness of you. You'll experience this truth especially in your prayer time. In a strict sense, you can't pray well with a heart that holds anything against anyone—a heart that feels offended or can't forget an offense.

You want to be able to prevail in prayer; you want to move mountains. So release offenders from the heart.

FORGIVE! Notice the word "GIVE" in FORGIVE. When you forgive, you give someone a gift. You waive a penalty. And you give yourself the gift of grudge-free living. When you withhold forgiveness, you not only refuse to offer someone what God has freely given you, but you also hurt yourself. Unforgiveness bears down on your heart. It gets in the way of spiritual growth. God knows it is not easy to forgive wrongs, but He isn't asking you to do something without giving you the grace to do it. Ask Him for the ability to forgive freely as you have been forgiven. He's the Master of the impossible. And He'll give you mastery as you clothe yourself with the nature of Christ.

~A Statement of Forgiveness~

I forgive (insert name) for (list wrongs against you). I take authority over Satan in the name of the Lord Jesus Christ and by the power of His resurrected life. I take back the ground I have allowed the enemy to take in my life because of my attitude toward (insert name). And I give the ground or territory of my heart back to my Lord Jesus Christ.

FORGIVING MADE EASIER

One Bible story which I've ever remembered since childhood is the story about Peter asking Jesus how many times he should forgive someone who has sinned against him. Jesus replies with an absurd number of times God commands to forgive offenders: "seventy times seven." And then Jesus follows with a parable about forgiveness. Read Matthew 18:21-35. As a child, I thought, "Wow, 490 times! That's a lot of forgiving." But, that's the point. You are never to stop forgiving. Jesus makes it very clear that unless you forgive others, your Father in heaven will not forgive you. Matthew 6:15 says, "But if you do not forgive others their trespasses [their reckless and willful sins, leaving them, letting them go, and giving up resentment] neither will your Father forgive you your trespasses." (AMPC)

Romans 12: 17–21 states, "Repay no one evil for evil, but give thought to do what is honorable in the sight of all. If possible, so far as it depends on you, live peaceably with all. Beloved, never avenge yourselves, but leave it to the wrath of God, for it is written, 'Vengeance is mine, I will repay, says the Lord.' To the contrary, 'if your enemy is hungry, feed him; if he is thirsty, give him something to drink; for by so doing you will heap burning coals on his head.' Do not be overcome by evil, but overcome evil with good." (ESV)

Saul was a man who avenged himself. He chased David, a man of honor, for fourteen years and murdered the priests and their families. It is "righteous" for God to avenge His servants; it is "unrighteous" for God's servants to avenge themselves.

Help comes from the Lord. Dennis and Dr. Jen Clark, co-authors of the book *Deep Relief Now*, write:

> If prayer begins with an open heart, then forgiveness must also start with the heart. And this means forgiveness starts with your emotions as well as with your thoughts and choices. As soon as God is in the loop, he can forgive through you. Christ the Forgiver lives inside each of us. So you have to stop trying to forgive and simply yield to Christ the Forgiver in your heart, allowing Him to forgive through you. Forgiving this way brings release.
>
> ~ Confession of Faith

> "And be not conformed to this age, but be ye transformed by the renewing of your soul (thoughts and recesses of the mind, will, and emotions) that ye may experience what is that good and well pleasing and perfect will of God." (Romans 12:2 JUB)

FREE TO OBEY

Knowing God will always forgive you does not mean you are free to sin. Romans 6:14-16 says,

> "But you are free under God's favor and mercy. Does this mean that now we can go ahead and sin and not worry about it? (For our salvation does not depend on keeping the law but on receiving God's grace!) Of course not! Don't you realize that you can choose your own master? You can choose sin (with death) or else obedience (with acquittal)." (TLB)

The release of grace is not meant to encourage sin. Rather, the call is to live in obedience. Is there an area of sin in your life that you struggle with? Repent. Change direction. Live a life of ongoing repentance. Acts 3:19 says,

> "Now change your mind and attitude to God and turn to him so he can cleanse away your sins and send you wonderful times of refreshment from the presence of the Lord." (TLB)

Don't treat sin casually on the ground that you know you will be forgiven. Instead, ask God to strengthen you and help you stop committing the sin.

~Prayer~

Father, thank You for the gift of eternal life in Christ. I have received Your great gift of love and mercy. Thank You, Lord, for your generous grace that frees me to obey You. Thank You for the love manifested through Your Son, Jesus—the love that's behind all Your commands. Your love abounds. Jesus, I love You. Amen.

GROW IN PATIENCE

Hebrews 6:12 prescribes patience:

> *"In order that you may not grow disinterested and become [spiritual] sluggards, but imitators, behaving as do those who through faith (by their leaning of the entire personality on God in Christ in absolute trust and confidence in His power, wisdom, and goodness) and by practice of patient endurance and waiting are [now] inheriting the promises." (AMPC)*

Patience is part of the fruit of the spirit. Galatians 5:22–23 says, "But the fruit of the Spirit is love, joy, peace, forbearance, kindness, goodness, faithfulness, gentleness and self-control. Against such things there is no law." (NIV) The Amplified adds the fruit is "the work which His presence within accomplishes."

When you're impatient, it's an act of the flesh without life. See Galatians 5:19. What the Spirit brings forth is fruit full of life. Patience is commonly defined as the capacity to accept or tolerate delay, trouble, or suffering without getting angry or upset. Patience originates from God.

> *"These things that were written in the Scriptures so long ago are to teach us patience and to encourage us so that we will look forward expectantly to the time when God will conquer sin and death. May God who gives patience, steadiness, and encouragement help you to live in complete harmony with each other—each with the attitude of Christ toward the other. And then all of us can praise the Lord together with one voice, giving glory to God, the Father of our Lord Jesus Christ." (Romans 15:4-6 TLB)*

~Confession~

Patience suffers long with difficult people. Love waits as long as necessary like a candle that has a very long wick and is therefore prepared to burn a long time. It is ready to forbear and wait patiently until the one finally comes around, makes progress, and changes.

WEARY NOT

Hebrews 12:3 says,

> *"Just think of Him Who endured from sinners such grievous opposition and bitter hostility against Himself [reckon up and consider it all in comparison with your trials], so that you may not grow weary or exhausted, losing heart and relaxing and fainting in your minds." (AMPC)*

2 Peter 1:6 says patience is a product of self-control and is part of godliness.

> *"Now for this very reason, making every effort, add to your faith virtue; and to virtue, knowledge; and to knowledge, self-control; and to self-control, patience; and to patience, godliness." (TLV)*

Hebrews 10:36 calls for patience: "Patient endurance is what you need now, so that you will continue to do God's will. Then you will receive all that he has promised." (NLT) And Hebrews 6:12 calls for diligence, "so that you will not be sluggish, but imitators of those who through faith and patience inherit the promises." (NASB) Abraham is the great example: "And so, having patiently waited, he obtained the promise." (Hebrews 6:15 NASB) And Christ demonstrated all patience. See 2 Thessalonians 3:5. Your patience pleases God and results in blessings from God on your life.

As a believer, you must consider Jesus at all times. He faced much opposition while He was on earth fulfilling the plans and purposes of His Father. Jesus endured opposition and hostility from sinners so you today won't grow weary and lose heart. No matter what you are facing today, you will be able to endure. You will be able to win. Keep your eyes on Jesus!

~Prayer~

Lord, only You know my future and what I must endure. Because you endured much hostility and opposition from sinners, I can, too. Thank You for adequately equipping me for the journey of life. I can win in the face of opposition. I can overcome because You overcame for me. In Jesus' name.

A DIRECTED LIFE

Proverbs 3:5-6 directs,

> "Lean on, trust in, and be confident in the Lord with all your heart and mind and do not rely on your own insight or understanding. In all your ways know, recognize, and acknowledge Him, and He will direct and make straight and plain your paths." (AMPC)

Today I am encouraging you to have faith in God and not in your own thinking or natural reasoning. Trust the leadership of the Holy Spirit. Live a directed life. Doing what God says to do is obedience. Expecting God to do what He said He will do is faith. Take in Hebrews 11:6, "But without faith it is impossible to please and be satisfactory to Him. For whoever would come near to God must [necessarily] believe that God exists and that He is the rewarder of those who earnestly and diligently seek Him [out]." (AMPC)

In Mark 2:6–8, Jesus confronts reasoning:

> *"Now some of the scribes were sitting there, holding a dialogue with themselves as they questioned in their hearts, Why does this Man talk like this? He is blaspheming! Who can forgive sin [remove guilt, remit the penalty, and bestow righteousness instead] except God alone? And at once Jesus, becoming fully aware in His spirit that they thus debated within themselves, said to them, 'Why do you argue (debate, reason) about all this in your hearts?'" (AMPC)*

The religious leaders of Jesus' day were saying unkind things about Jesus in their hearts but not out loud. They were asking questions about Jesus within themselves. Jesus became aware of their arguments, debate, and reasoning in His spirit and called these things to their attention. Be aware that trying to reason everything out is a problem. The practice of reasoning is a serious matter that needs to be dealt with in the way that Jesus dealt with it in the hearts of would-be followers. Ask God to help you stop reasoning. Begin to live by faith. Lean on and trust in Him and not on your own understanding. Proverbs 3:7 commands, "Be not wise in your own eyes." (AMPC) You need God.

~Prayer~

Dear Lord, I cannot run my own life and do a good job without You. I need You. I need Your help. I need Your direction. I trust You to direct my life. Thank You, now. In Jesus' name.

REASONING IS NOT FAITH

Proverbs 3:1 says, "My son, forget not my law or teaching, but let your heart keep my commandments." (AMPC) Proverbs 3:3 adds, "Let not mercy and kindness [shutting out all hatred and selfishness] and truth [shutting out all deliberate hypocrisy or falsehood] forsake you; bind them about your neck, write them upon the tablet of your heart." (AMPC) Also note Colossians 3:9–12:

> "Do not lie to one another, for you have stripped off the old (unregenerate) self with its evil practices, and have clothed yourselves with the new [spiritual self], which is [ever in the process of being] renewed and remolded into [fuller and more perfect knowledge upon] knowledge after the image (the likeness) of Him Who created it. [In this new creation all distinctions vanish.] There is no room for and there can be neither Greek nor Jew, circumcised nor uncircumcised, [nor difference between nations whether alien] barbarians or Scythians [who are the most savage of all], nor slave or free man; but Christ is all and in all [everything and everywhere, to all men, without distinction of person].Clothe yourselves therefore, as God's own chosen ones (His own picked representatives), [who are] purified and holy and well-beloved [by God Himself, by putting on behavior marked by] tenderhearted pity and mercy, kind feeling, a lowly opinion of yourselves, gentle ways, [and] patience [which is tireless and long-suffering, and has the power to endure whatever comes, with good temper]." (AMPC)

Proverbs 3:5–7 states,

> "Lean on, trust in, and be confident in the Lord with all your heart and mind and do not rely on your own insight or understanding. In all your ways know, recognize, and acknowledge Him, and He will direct and make straight and plain your paths. Be not wise in your own eyes; reverently fear and worship the Lord and turn [entirely] away from evil." (AMPC)

You cannot run your own life and do a good job without His help. You are designed to abide in the Vine —the Lord—as your source. See John 15. Proverbs 3:6–7 encourages faith in God vs. faith in your own thinking or reasoning. When you reason out everything, you have a hard time with faith because walking by natural reasoning is not walking by faith. And Hebrews 11:6 says, "Without faith it is impossible to please him." (ESV)

~Prayer~

Dear Lord, help me to stop reasoning and start living by faith, leaning on You and trusting in You. I choose not to trust in my own understanding. I trust You, Lord. In Jesus' name. So be it!

PLACE YOUR CONFIDENCE SOLELY IN CHRIST

Proverbs 3:26 is a key verse:

> *"For the Lord shall be your confidence, firm and strong, and shall keep your foot from being caught [in a trap or some hidden danger]." (AMPC)*

As a believer you should not place your confidence in education, your good looks, any position you hold in society, property you own, your natural gifts or talents, your abilities, accomplishments or the opinions of others. The Father is saying, "no more," to reliance on these things. It's time to let go of all the fleshly things you've held to so firmly for so long. It is time to put your trust and confidence in Christ and Christ, alone.

> *"Truly I tell you, if anyone says to this mountain, 'Go, throw yourself into the sea,' and does not doubt in their heart but believes that what they say will happen, it will be done for them. Therefore I tell you, whatever you ask for in prayer, believe that you have received it, and it will be yours. (Mark 11:23–25)*

~Prayer~

Dear Lord, forgive me for not trusting You in all areas of my life. I assumed I could handle certain things myself. Thank You for being my confidence, my firm and strong Rock. Thank You for keeping my foot from being caught in the net of the enemy. Thank You, now. In Jesus' name.

DO NOT HATE INSTRUCTION

Proverbs 5 warns against the situation of verses 12 and 13,

> *"And you say, How I hated instruction and discipline, and my heart despised reproof! I have not obeyed the voice of my teachers nor submitted and consented to those who instructed me." (AMPC)*

Say instead, "I do not hate instruction. I am teachable." 1 Corinthians 8:2 reveals, "Anyone who claims to know all the answers doesn't really know very much." (NLT)

Do not use the words "hate" and "despise." You are not supposed to hate anything but sin. Hate only what God hates: sin. The enemy of your soul uses the feelings of dread and hatred to deceive. And dread is a close relative of fear. Choose to have a heart that despises no one and nothing.

~Prayer~

Lord, I repent of any hatred in my heart especially towards instruction and reproof. I repent of hating anyone or anything. I replace these negative thoughts and emotions now with truth. I ask that You forgive me and replace my hatred with Your love and grace. I will not have an attitude of despising things in my heart. I will choose to let You fill my heart with Your love and grace. In Jesus' name I pray.

HATE WHAT GOD HATES

You can learn a lot from the ant. Proverbs 6:6–11 says,

> *"Go to the ant, you sluggard; consider her ways and be wise! —Which, having no chief, overseer, or ruler, Provides her food in the summer and gathers her supplies in the harvest. How long will you sleep, O sluggard? When will you arise out of your sleep? Yet a little sleep, a little slumber, a little folding of the hands to lie down and sleep—So will your poverty come like a robber or one who travels [with slowly but surely approaching steps] and your want like an armed man [making you helpless]." (AMPC)*

God commends the ant but says He hates certain human traits:

> *"These six things the Lord hates, indeed, seven are an abomination to Him: A proud look [the spirit that makes one overestimate himself and underestimate others], a lying tongue, and hands that shed innocent blood, A heart that manufactures wicked thoughts and plans, feet that are swift in running to evil, A false witness who breathes out lies [even under oath], and he who sows discord among his brethren." (Proverbs 6:16-19 AMPC)*

The answer is to live by God's Word and store it in the heart to keep you from sin as Psalm 119:11 states. Proverbs 6:23 says, "For the commandment is a lamp, and the whole teaching [of the law] is light, and reproofs of discipline are the way of life." (AMPC) Psalm 19:8 says of the Lord's precepts: "The precepts of the Lord are right, rejoicing the heart; the commandment of the Lord is pure and bright, enlightening the eyes." (AMPC)

~Prayer~

Father, help me to live by Your Word so You will be glorified and I will enjoy Your blessings. In Jesus' name.

PRESS ON

Philippians 3:13-14 encourages pressing on:

> "Brethren, I do not count myself to have apprehended; but one thing I do, forgetting those things which are behind and reaching forward to those things which are ahead, I press toward the goal for the prize of the upward call of God in Christ Jesus." (NKJV)

The enemy wants you to focus on your past instead of your future. He wants you to look at how far you still have to go vs. how far you have come in the Lord. So focus on your strengths in God and not personal weaknesses. Count your victories and not your losses. Focus on your joys instead of problems. Press ahead in response to God's upward call. Forget the things that lie behind you. Press on; press on. You can do it!

~Prayer~

Lord, help me to keep Your works before me. Help me to magnify them. I do not believe the lies of the enemy of my soul. I choose to press forward. I respond by faith now to the upward call of the Lord in my life. I am a person of the present and future and not a person of the past. I am now in a good place of victory. I am blessed. In Jesus' name.

SECTION FOUR

UNRESERVED LOVE

Everywhere Jesus went, people saw God's love manifested. Every time He helped someone, every time He delivered someone from demonic powers, and every time He worked a miracle, people saw the love of God in action. You are called to live your life the same way. In fact, if you ever allow yourself to get distracted from your primary purpose of giving out Christ's love—if the business of life gets in the way—even if that business concerns the work of the Lord, you will miss the mark. Whatever you do should be so permeated by the love of God that you should be able to say of yourself as Jesus said of Himself,

> *"If you have seen me, you have seen the Father." (See John 14:7.)*

In other words, "If you have seen me, you have seen love." Keep this true truth in mind as you study the section that follows: Unreserved Love.

PURE IN HEART

Matthew 5:8 promises, "Blessed are the pure in heart, for they shall see God." (ESV) What does it mean to be pure-hearted and powerful in perception? A person with a pure heart is someone who wholeheartedly serves God as he or she flows with His unreserved love. That person is pure in heart toward God and man. These qualities alone make such ones as powerful. And God is seeking ones who are pure in heart. If you are pure in heart in seeking God, you will see God. Seeing God is your reward. This blessing is for today in your life and for the coming age.

Psalm 24:3–4 asks, "Who can climb Mount God? Who can scale the holy north-face? Only the clean-handed, only the pure-hearted; Men who won't cheat, women who won't seduce." (MSG) And David says of God in Psalm 51:6, "And yes, you want truth in the most hidden places; you teach me wisdom in the most secret space." (CEB) Having a pure heart means having truth in your inner being. It means paying attention to your thoughts because from your thoughts come your words, emotions, attitudes, and motives.

God will not bless actions done out of wrong motives or anything else impure in the heart. Luke 6:45 teaches, "A good person produces good from the good treasury of the inner self... The inner self overflows with words that are spoken." (CEB) Purity of heart does not come naturally in most people. It is something that comes with "working out your salvation." (See Philippians 2:12.) The Word teaches you to desire purity. It is God's will for you to sow to purity of heart through taking in the Word and letting His blood cleanse you.

Take bananas for example. To consume the valuable fruit, typically you peel the banana from the bottom where it was attached to the stem in the middle of the plant. Bananas grow from the stem upward. The bottom is actually the top. You could sit in a banana tree and eat bananas straight from the source. You'd open them from the non-stem end. I have always opened them from the non-stem end and used the stem as a handle. Either way, you separate the worthless peel from the valuable fruit. God knows how best to peel you.

~Meditation~

Consider the aim of your heart. You face paying a price to have a pure heart, but you will gain a reward. Don't pull back from letting God do a deep, purifying work in you. You may not always feel comfortable with the truth the Holy Spirit brings you, but if you will do your part and face the truth—if you will accept it and allow it to change you—God will bless you. It's what's inside your heart that matters most.

DISARMING WEAPON

1 Corinthians 13:4-8 portrays love.

> *"Love is patient, love is kind. It does not envy, it does not boast, it is not proud. It does not dishonor others, it is not self-seeking, it is not easily angered, it keeps no record of wrongs. Love does not delight in evil but rejoices with the truth. It always protects, always trusts, always hopes, always perseveres. Love never fails." (NIV)*

Love is a weapon that disarms—a spiritual weapon in your arsenal. It cannot be overcome. Love breaks down defenses and walls. I declare we are going to get such a revelation of what this kind of love looks like that we will walk in it and break down the forces of the enemy. In Jesus' name. Luke 6:45 teaches,

> *"A good person produces good from the good treasury of the inner self... The inner self overflows with words that are spoken." (CEB)*

Martin Luther King, Jr. stated the need for love:

Power without love is reckless and abusive, and love without power is sentimental and anemic. Power at its best is love implementing the demands of justice, and justice at its best is power correcting everything that stands against love.

~Declaration and Prayer~

Mercy conquers judgment. Mercy upon mercy upon mercy! Lord, conquer me by Your mercy, and let me conquer by Your mercy and with Your love. I want to be able to release Your love to those around me who are so love-starved. Help me to walk out the revelation of Your mercy and love. Help me understand how to release love. Speak to me today concerning love.

AN UNDERSTANDING HEART

Proverbs 2:1–5 teaches about the necessity of understanding. It also speaks of reward.

> "My son, if you accept my words and store up my commands within you, listening closely to wisdom and directing your heart to understanding; furthermore, if you call out to insight and lift your voice to understanding, if you seek it like silver and search for it like hidden treasure, then you will understand the fear of the Lord and discover the knowledge of God." (HCSB)

You need to seek understanding of God's Word and will as concerns yourself and other people. The focus must be on the Holy Spirit and gaining an understanding of others in order to minister to people. I must have an understanding heart. And how can I attain this if I do not have a clue about their struggles and hurts?

~Prayer~

Lord, keep me focused on You and the leadership of the Holy Spirit. The Spirit will give me words of knowledge to clue me in on the people before me. Help me, Lord, to be a blessing to everyone I encounter, especially my family and the family of God. I thank You now. In Jesus' name. Proverbs 1:7 declares, "The fear of the Lord is the beginning of knowledge." (HCSB) Proverbs 2:6 states, "For the Lord gives wisdom; from His mouth come knowledge and understanding." (HCSB)

SERVANTHOOD

John 13:3–5 depicts the servanthood of the Lord:

> *"[That] Jesus, knowing (fully aware) that the Father had put everything into His hands, and that He had come from God and was [now] returning to God, got up from supper, took off His garments, and taking a [servant's] towel, He fastened it around His waist. Then He poured water into the washbasin and began to wash the disciples' feet and to wipe them with the [servant's] towel with which He was girded." (AMPC)*

Jesus washed His disciples' feet as an act of servanthood. He acted to show them how very much He loved them. Pride never kept the Lord from demonstrating His love. In His culture, people's sandals did not protect their feet from the dirt on the road. And servants, not masters, were supposed to wash feet. But Jesus, who knew He was the Lord, became the servant of all. He washed all of the disciples' feet. In verses 12–15, the Lord says follow His example:

> *"So when He had finished washing their feet and had put on His garments and had sat down again, He said to them, do you understand what I have done to you? You call Me the Teacher (Master) and the Lord, and you are*

> right in doing so, for that is what I am. If I then, your Lord and Teacher (Master), have washed your feet, you ought [it is your duty, you are under obligation, you owe it] to wash one another's feet. For I have given you this as an example, so that you should do [in your turn] what I have done to you." (AMPC)

Wash one another's feet. You must be willing to serve one another rather than be served by others to be a part of Jesus and the Body.

~Prayer~

Lord, help me to serve others vs. merely letting them serve me. Help me to treat others with utmost respect and be good to them that You be glorified in my life. In Jesus' name I pray.

TAPPING THE SOURCE

Study 1 John 3:16:

> "By this we come to know (progressively to recognize, to perceive, to understand) the [essential] love: that He laid down His [own] life for us; and we ought to lay [our] lives down for [those who are our] brothers [in Him]." (AMPC)

From where does love come? Love springs from God. God is love 1 John states. If you love your fellow man and your brothers and sisters in Christ, you know you are born of God. Loving others causes you to progressively know and understand, perceive, and recognize who God really is. You know you are in the light when you live in the truth that you are to love your fellows. The Bible says a believer ought to lay down his life for the brothers and sisters in the Lord.

~Prayer~

Father, may my life be hid in Christ. May the love of Your Son be manifest in my life. Show me how to love my fellow man as You have loved me so I may clearly come to know and recognize who You really are—Love! In Jesus' name.

COMMIT TO LOVE

John 13:34–35 are the verses to look at:

> "I give you a new commandment: that you should love one another. Just as I have loved you, so you too should love one another. By this shall all [men] know that you are My disciples, if you love one another [if you keep on showing love among yourselves]." (AMPC)

What does it mean to commit to love? It can mean to bind yourself to giving love as by a promise or by a pledge. Love people by making them feel valuable. See others through the eyes of God. Ask Him how He sees the different ones. Making people feel valuable won't cost you any money. However, this practice will give them something more valuable than anything money can buy. Commit to build others by complimenting at least three people a day.

~Prayer~

Lord, I ask for Your strength and power so I can make a difference in this world. I want to be Your disciple so others will see Your love manifested through me. In Jesus' name.

GIVING OUT LOVE

It isn't always easy to live together with other Christians in harmony and love, but the Bible proclaims it is possible and doable. In Paul's letter to the Romans, he gives some helpful tips on flowing outwardly in the Spirit in God's love for others. Romans 15:1–2 admonishes,

> *"Now we who are strong ought to bear the weaknesses of those without strength and not just please ourselves. Each of us is to please his neighbor for his good, to his edification." (NASB)*

Verses 5–7 call for unity:

> *"May the God who inspires men to endure, and gives them a Father's care, give you a mind united towards one another because of your common loyalty to Jesus Christ. And then, as one man, you will sing from the heart the praises of God the Father of our Lord Jesus Christ. So open your hearts to one another as Christ has opened his heart to you, and God will be glorified." (PHILLIPS)*

The key is receiving from God first. You can open yourself to the Father's affection, attention, and care. And you can receive the mind of the Spirit.

~Prayer~

Father, let me so receive Your love, and let me so function in the mind of the Spirit that my heart stays open and in unity with my brothers and sisters in Christ. Let me love with Your heart.

LOVE COVERS THE WRONGS OF OTHERS

> "Hatred stirs up contentions, but love covers all transgressions." (Proverbs 10:12 AMPC)

Love covers all wrongs. Above all else, draw on God's extreme strength and have unfailing love for one another. For love forgives and disregards the offenses of others. Love will outlast failure. You must freely admit to the Father that you have missed the mark—you have sinned. Confess your sins. He is faithful and just, true to His nature and promises. He will forgive you. And remember, He forgives others.

Remember, where there is hatred, strife is stirred up. When believers bear with each other, peace and harmony are preserved.

~Prayer~

Dear Father, You are good, and Your mercy endures forever. Your blessings crown the head of the righteous, but violence overwhelms the mouth of the wicked. (Proverbs 10:6) May I display love mercy and grace to others.

DOING GOOD

Jesus is the example in Acts 10:38:

> "How God anointed and consecrated Jesus of Nazareth with the [Holy] Spirit and with strength and ability and power; how He went about doing good and, in particular, curing all who were harassed and oppressed by [the power of] the devil, for God was with Him." (AMPC)

Note Jesus went about doing good. His main business was to travel from place to place doing good. And God was with Jesus. The miracles He did could only be performed by God with Him. You, too, are to walk with God like Jesus. Today be mindful to be a blessing to others.

~Prayer~

Dear Lord, help me to put on love as I put on Christ. Help me to reach out to others on purpose. May I watch and pray for opportunities to touch lives. May I spy out the land for God. In Jesus' name.

LOVE SEES NEEDS

Love is 1 John 3:17:

> *"But if anyone has this world's goods (resources for sustaining life) and sees his brother and fellow believer in need, yet closes his heart of compassion against him, how can the love of God live and remain in him?" (AMPC)*

This verse has an important question to ponder in your heart. This verse is saying you can decide to open or close your heart of compassion when you see a need. But if you close your heart of compassion when you see a need, the love of God cannot stay alive and remain in you. You have to remember God is love.

~Prayer~

I choose today to be aware of those with whom I come in contact. I choose to show compassion and meet needs. I will value them as ones for whom You died—ones You love dearly. In Jesus' name.

GIVE

Luke 6:38 prescribes,

> *"Give, and [gifts] will be given to you; good measure, pressed down, shaken together, and running over, will they pour into [the pouch formed by] the bosom [of your robe and used as a bag]. For with the measure you deal out [with the measure you use when you confer benefits on others], it will be measured back to you." (AMPC)*

Humans live backward from the way God designed them to live. They live for themselves, and they are never satisfied. The design is to live for God first and then for others. There is a secret to life: what you give away comes back to you multiplied many times over. Giving, not getting, is the way.

~Prayer~

Father, I ask You to empower me to live in a forward way and not backward. Giving and not getting is the way. I choose to live in this life so I can manifest God's love to others. Thank you, Jesus.

LOVE SACRIFICES

1 Corinthians 13:5 says of love:

> *"Love does not behave rudely, does not seek its own, is not provoked, thinks no evil." (NKJV)*

In other words, love sacrifices. To sacrifice means to give up something you might prefer to keep. In the Greek, the original language of the New Testament, the word sacrifice means an act of offering or the thing that is offered.

94 | LOVE'S AIM

Love does not insist on its own way. Love often requires you to sacrifice doing things your way. Remember Jesus' life as the greatest example of continual sacrifice. The Word urges believers:

> "With eyes wide open to the mercies of God, I beg you, my brothers, as an act of intelligent worship, to give him your bodies, as a living sacrifice, consecrated to him and acceptable by him." (Romans 12:1 PHILLIPS)

The natural tendency is to keep and not give. In Christ, you can give sacrificially.

~PRAYER~

Heavenly Father, give me Your strength so I can deny myself and sacrifice things in my life. Grace me that I can give up and give over and not hold onto my own way. Forgive me for not fully acknowledging the sacrifice that Jesus made in His life on earth and death on the cross. In Jesus' name.

THE SACRIFICE OF YOUR BODY

Romans 12:1 in the Amplified is thoroughgoing:

> "I appeal to you therefore, brethren, and beg of you in view of [all] the mercies of God, to make a decisive dedication of your bodies [presenting all your members and faculties] as a living sacrifice, holy (devoted, consecrated) and well pleasing to God, which is your reasonable (rational, intelligent) service and spiritual worship."

This verse speaks of dedicating your very body as a living sacrifice. It calls you to offer up all of your faculties to Him for His use. Wrong thinking about the self will not lead to right doing. The master word for the outward life of a Christian is sacrifice. Become an offering unto God. And such sacrifice involves two things: death to self and surrender to God.

~Prayer~

Lord, I offer You my heart, eyes, ears, mouth, hands, finances, gifts, time, energy and every ability. Use me to be a blessing anywhere and everywhere. Use me to be a blessing today. In Jesus' name.

WHATEVER IT TAKES

1 Corinthians 2:1–2 reveals the apostle Paul's mindset:

> *"As for myself, brethren, when I came to you, I did not come proclaiming to you the testimony and evidence or mystery and secret of God [concerning what He has done through Christ for the salvation of men] in lofty words of eloquence or human philosophy and wisdom; For I resolved to know nothing (to be acquainted with nothing, to make a display of the knowledge of nothing, and to be conscious of nothing) among you except Jesus Christ (the Messiah) and Him crucified." (AMPC)*

Paul adds in 4–5,

> *"And my language and my message were not set forth in persuasive (enticing and plausible) words of wisdom, but they were in demonstration of the [Holy] Spirit and power [[d]a proof by the Spirit and power of God, operating on me and stirring in the minds of my hearers the most holy emotions and thus persuading them], So that your faith might not rest in the wisdom of men (human philosophy), but in the power of God." (AMPC)*

The apostle adjusted himself around people. He became whatever people needed him to be. He did whatever it took to win them to Christ. He showed love to them. Though Paul was highly educated, he never belittled anyone. He chose to be acquainted with nothing except Jesus Christ and Christ crucified. Today can be your day to make others feel accepted and valued and lifted up by the love of God.

~Prayer~

Thank You, Lord. Today I look forward to encounters with others where I can display the love of Christ. I look forward to encounters where I can put others first and listen to them as they talk and share their dreams or challenges. Like Paul, I am acquainted with nothing except Jesus Christ the Messiah and Him crucified. This mindset is what it takes. In His name: Jesus.

TELLING OTHERS ABOUT JESUS

The world desperately needs to see real love in action. Have you ever thought about what's the best way to tell others about Jesus? In John 13:34, Jesus gives the answer:

> *"I give you a new commandment: that you should love one another. Just as I have loved you, so you too should love one another." (AMPC)*

Just love them like they are no matter how they act or live. Live out the same love you've received from the Lord. John 13:35 makes it plain that all men will know you are a disciple of Jesus Christ if you keep showing love to believers. Include those yet to believe.

> *"This is how everyone will recognize that you are my disciples—when they see the love you have for each other." (John 13:35 MSG)*

The Living Bible adds,

> *"Your strong love for each other will PROVE to the world that you are my disciples."*

~Prayer~

Lord, give me all I need to live out the selfless, sacrificial love I have received from You. Help me to extend that love to those who have not yet trusted in You as Lord and Savior. I want to reflect who You are Jesus and what You are all about. May my life speak loudly of You, Lord. In His name—the sweetest name I know. Amen. So be it!

EXTENDING LOVE TO THE LOST

Do you have a hard time telling others about Jesus? John 13:35 in the Amplified says "Keep on showing love." Your actions will speak loudly about who Jesus is. 1 Corinthians 13:4–8 says of love,

> "Love endures long and is patient and kind; love never is envious nor boils over with jealousy, is not boastful or vainglorious, does not display itself haughtily. It is not conceited (arrogant and inflated with pride); it is not rude (unmannerly) and does not act unbecomingly. Love (God's love in us) does not insist on its own rights or its own way, for it is not self-seeking; it is not touchy or fretful or resentful; it takes no account of the evil done to it [it pays no attention to a suffered wrong]. It does not rejoice at injustice and unrighteousness, but rejoices when right and truth prevail. Love bears up under anything and everything that comes, is ever ready to believe the best of every person, its hopes are fadeless under all circumstances, and it endures everything [without weakening]. Love never fails [never fades out or becomes obsolete or comes to an end]. As for prophecy (the gift of interpreting the divine will and purpose), it will be fulfilled and pass away; as for tongues, they will be destroyed and cease; as for knowledge, it will pass away [it will lose its value and be superseded by truth]." (AMPC)

Love should be number one on your spiritual priority list. You should study love, pray about love, and develop the fruit of love by practicing loving others. God is love so when you abide in Him according to John 15, you will walk in love. He is your source.

~Prayer~

Lord, I want to love like You love. Thank You for Your love. Make me a student of love. I commit my life to love because You are love. Thank You for everyone with whom I come in contact. Let Your love flow through me to them. In Jesus' name.

LOVE GIVES UP THINGS

God gave up His Son for love. John 3:16 states,

> *"For God so greatly loved and dearly prized the world that He [even] gave up His only begotten (unique) Son, so that whoever believes in (trusts in, clings to, relies on) Him shall not perish (come to destruction, be lost) but have eternal (everlasting) life." (AMPC)*

What does it really mean to give up something or someone you love? God the Father set the living example for the world when He gave up His only begotten, unique Son, Jesus. He bestowed this great gift of love on the entire human race. He yielded His Son to the whole world. He so dearly prized and loved the world that He gave. Love gives up things.

~Prayer~

Thank You, God, for loving me so much that You gave Your unique and only begotten Son Jesus to die for me. Thank You for giving up the Son You love so I might have life through Him. Amen.

THE WORLD IS LOOKING FOR LOVE

1 John 4:8 states the truth,

> *"He who does not love has not become acquainted with God [does not and never did know Him], for God is love." (AMPC)*

The world is looking for something real—something tangible. If you are born again and know God, you can offer the answer:

> *"Christ in you, the hope of glory." (Colossians 1:27 NIV)*

Christ is the only hope of glory to the world. People around you are searching. Their hearts are crying out to God though sometimes they are unaware that it's God for whom they are searching.

~Prayer~

Dear Lord, help me to show those around me the hope and the love that come from knowing Christ in me, the hope of glory. I have God's love in my heart; I have what those in the world seek. Thank You for open doors. Thank You for encounters with those in need of Your love. In Jesus' name I pray!

> *"That I might fully declare God's word—that sacred mystery . . . Christ in you! Yes, Christ in you bringing with him the hope of all glorious things to come. So, naturally, we proclaim Christ! We warn everyone we meet, and we teach everyone we can, all that we know about him, so that, if possible, we may bring every man up to his full maturity in Christ. This is what I am working at all the time, with all the strength that God gives me." (Colossians 1:27-29 PHILLIPS)*

FOR LEADERS

As a leader you must develop people so they can serve God and do what He has called them to do. Jesus set forth the standard for Christian leadership when He washed His disciples' feet. Leaders are appointed to serve like He did. Although there are similarities in the roles leaders play in the natural and the spiritual, those in spiritual leadership have a much higher call. To be an effective spiritual leader, you must know the standards of God and then follow them. The order is move in love and give of yourself to others that the Kingdom of God is built and God's plan is fulfilled on earth. This highest way of love the Lord sets before you.

JESUS' IDENTITY IN FULLNESS

Jesus is the premier example of a man (and a leader) loving God with all of His soul by living with a right and true identity. His identity is grounded in love and humility instead of in the response of the people to His ministry. His humility was most clearly expressed in history when He became a man and died on the cross.

Jesus has two natures, being fully God and fully man. He was never less than God, but lived on earth as though He was never more than a man. Being in the form of God, He had the ability to use divine power to influence people during His earthly ministry. Yet, He only used this power when He was led by the Spirit. He lived as every other godly person by waiting (and depending) on the Spirit's leadership. He emptied Himself of the right to take the initiative to use the fullness of power.

Jesus did not consider it robbery (KJV) to be equal to God in privilege and honor. This has been applied two ways. First, Jesus would not have taken anything from God by insisting on enjoying the privileges equal to the Father. These were rightfully His by virtue of being God. Secondly, He did not take anything for Himself as He refused the privileges of being treated as equal to God.

He did not insist on His rights to live free from persecution, pain, and humiliation. When one has the power to create the heavens and the earth, why should He ever be hungry or rejected? In denying Himself of His rightful privileges by living as a bondservant, He did not deny His true identity, but was being true to Himself.

JESUS' IDENTITY IN HUMILITY

An important portrait of Jesus is found in Isaiah 53:

> "He had no special beauty or form [majesty] to make us notice him; there was nothing in his appearance to make us desire him. He was hated [despised] and rejected by people. He had much pain [A man of pain/suffering/sorrows] and suffering [one who knew/was acquainted with pain/grief]. People would not even look at [turned their backs on; hid their faces from] him. He was hated [despised], and we didn't even notice him [or did not esteem him]." (EXB)

Consider the imperfect analogy of having one hundred billion dollars without ever using it for yourself or even mentioning it once throughout your life. You would naturally want a few people to know about it because it would change the way they related to you. But not so with Jesus. Jesus related to people as a servant instead of as a powerful and influential man who was rich.

What was most important to Him was to tell the Father's story and to enrich the lives of people by dying for them. If His core identity had been in having power, then His incarnation would have been a denial of His true self. For all eternity, He delights in humility. It was not something He was only while on earth. It is something that He is. His humility did not begin at the incarnation.

JESUS' IDENTITY IN SERVANTHOOD

Jesus lived to serve. He went low. John 13:3–5 gives the proof:

> "Jesus knew that the Father had given him power over everything [placed everything into his hands] and that he had come from God and was going

> back to God. So during the meal [from supper] Jesus stood up and took off his outer clothing. Taking a towel, he wrapped it around his waist. Then he poured water into a bowl and began to wash the followers' [disciples'] feet, drying [wiping] them with the towel that was wrapped around him. [This act was considered so demeaning by some people that they only allowed Gentile slaves to do it.]" (EXB)

Jesus emptied Himself of His reputation in the eyes of man. He embraced a lifestyle where everyone underestimated Him and His abilities. People never knew how superior His abilities were. When they saw Him, they saw nothing to distinguish Him. He was happy to be seen as an ordinary man without any special form (status) or comeliness (attractiveness).

JESUS' IDENTITY IN LOVE

In Philippians 2:6–8, you, as a leader, gain insight into how Jesus carried His heart before God and people.

> "Christ himself was like God in everything [Who, being in the form of God]. But he did not think that being equal with God was something to be used for his own benefit [or grasped; seized; held on to]. But he gave up his place with God and made himself nothing [emptied himself]. He became like [took the form of] a servant [slave; bondservant] and was born as a man [in the likeness of humanity/men]. And when he was living [being found in appearance/likeness] as a man [human being], he humbled himself and was fully obedient to God, even when that caused his [to the point of] death—death on a cross." (EXB)

Jesus did not serve to prove something, but to express the truth about Himself. It is precisely because Jesus is God that He served and gave freely to ungrateful men. (See Luke 6:35.) There was nothing un-Godlike about washing the disciples' feet. He was at home doing this.

You are to love God with all your soul by stewarding His calling and blessing on your life with a servant identity instead of in your influence and given abilities or in how big your business or ministry is. You are equally yoked to Jesus not by the size of your love, but by the "all" of your love. Though your "all" is small, the point is that it is your "all." He wants you to love (and serve) in the way He loves you. He gave all. Support

Nehemiah was a leader. Nehemiah saw success: "So we built the wall, and all [of it] was joined together to half its height, for the people had a heart and mind to work." (Nehemiah 4:6 AMPC) In verse 9, they prayed as they faced the enemy: "But because of them (the enemies) we made our prayer to our God and set a watch against them day and night." (AMPC)

If you are under attack as a leader, it's vitally important to have people in your life who will faithfully stand at your side through prayer and through other means of support. This is the time to intensify your prayers and increase your vigilance. In verses 4:14–18, you see the results,

> "I looked [them over] and rose up and said to the nobles and officials and the other people, Do not be afraid of the enemy; [earnestly] remember the Lord and imprint Him [on your minds], great and terrible, and [take from Him courage to] fight for your brethren, your sons, your daughters, your wives, and your homes. And when our enemies heard that their plot was known to us and that God had frustrated their purpose, we all returned to the wall, everyone to his work. And from that time forth, half of my servants worked at the task, and the other half held the spears, shields, bows, and coats of mail; and the leaders stood behind all the house of Judah. Those who built the wall and those who bore burdens loaded themselves so that everyone worked with one hand and held a weapon with the other hand, And every builder had his sword girded by his side, and so worked." (AMPC)

~Prayer~

Dear Lord, when opposition comes to me, I refuse to be upset! I will call to You, my God, and set a watch against the enemy through day and night. I will be thankful for those who stand with me in faithfulness and vigilant prayer. When my enemies come against me, You will frustrate their purposes, so I can return to the task You have given me. In Jesus' name.

A LEADER'S PRAYER

Nehemiah 1:5–11 reports a leader's prayer:

> "And I said, O Lord God of heaven, the great and terrible God, Who keeps covenant, loving-kindness, and mercy for those who love Him and keep His commandments, Let Your ear now be attentive and Your eyes open to listen to the prayer of Your servant which I pray before You day and night for the Israelites, Your servants, confessing the sins of the Israelites which we have sinned against You. Yes, I and my father's house have sinned. We have acted very corruptly against You and have not kept the commandments, statutes, and ordinances which You commanded Your servant Moses. Remember [earnestly] what You commanded Your servant Moses: If you transgress and are unfaithful, I will scatter you abroad among the nations; But if you return to Me and keep My commandments and do them, though your outcasts were in the farthest part of the heavens [the expanse of outer space], yet will I gather them from there and will bring them to the place in which I have chosen to set My Name. Now these are Your servants and Your people, whom You have redeemed by Your great power and by Your strong hand. O Lord, let Your ear be attentive to the prayer of Your servant and the prayer of Your servants who delight to revere and fear Your name (Your nature and attributes); and prosper, I pray You, Your servant this day and grant him mercy in the sight of this man. For I was cupbearer to the king." (AMPC)

Nehemiah waited for God to respond to his prayer for the Israelites. He prayed before the Lord day and night. Not only did he repent for the people, but also he repented for himself. He confessed his sins and failures to the Lord. He referenced the instructions of the Lord.

> *"Now this is the instruction, the laws, and the precepts which the Lord your God commanded me to teach you, that you might do them in the land to which you go to possess it, that you may [reverently] fear the Lord your God, you and your son and your son's son, and keep all His statutes and His commandments which I command you all the days of your life, and that your days may be prolonged. Hear therefore, O Israel, and be watchful to do them, that it may be well with you and that you may increase exceedingly, as the Lord, the God of your fathers, has promised you, in a land flowing with milk and honey. Hear, O Israel: the Lord our God is one Lord [the only Lord]. And you shall love the Lord your God with all your [mind and] heart and with your entire being and with all your might. And these words which I am commanding you this day shall be [first] in your [own] minds and hearts; [then] You shall whet and sharpen them so as to make them penetrate, and teach and impress them diligently upon the [minds and] hearts of your children, and shall talk of them when you sit in your house and when you walk by the way, and when you lie down and when you rise up. And you shall bind them as a sign upon your hand, and they shall be as frontlets (forehead bands) between your eyes. And you shall write them upon the doorposts of your house and on your gates."* (Deuteronomy 6:1-9 AMPC)

Nehemiah was confident that God would forgive the sins and failures and cleanse the people from all unrighteousness as He had promised. 1 John 1:9 says,

> *"If we [freely] admit that we have sinned and confess our sins, He is faithful and just (true to His own nature and promises) and will forgive our sins [dismiss our lawlessness] and [continuously] cleanse us from all unrighteousness [everything not in conformity to His will in purpose, thought, and action]."* (AMPC)

Ask yourself, do you give God time to answer when you pray? Or do you try to push ahead? You must know that when you pray according to Mark 11:22-24 believe that you receive and then you will have your answer. God will respond to your prayers in His perfect timing. Jesus said,

> *"Have faith in God. Truly, I say to you, whoever says to this mountain, 'Be taken up and thrown into the sea,' and does not doubt in his heart, but believes that what he says will come to pass, it will be done for him. Therefore I tell you, whatever you ask in prayer, believe that you have received it, and it will be yours." (Mark 11:22–24 ESV)*

~Prayer~

Lord, I thank You that Your good hand is upon me. I wait for Your timing when I pray. I already believe that I receive when I pray. I choose not to push ahead. I have the answer. Thank You for Your perfect timing. In Jesus' name.

BE SAVED THROUGH JESUS CHRIST

The Father, Son, and Holy Spirit have the love you need. As you've read these pages, you've read from the Bible, God's covenant of love with mankind.

The Father sent His Son, Jesus Christ, to die for you and make atonement or payment for your transgressions against a Holy God. By accepting the Risen Jesus into your heart as Lord and Savior you can be saved or rescued from your wayward ways and this present evil age. At salvation, you receive a new nature through a new birth. Christ comes to indwell you and Shepherd your life. He takes you from glory to glory as you surrender to Him. Salvation involves a "not my will but the Father's will" sojourn on the earth. Know that the Creator has a destiny for you—plans for you that are good, a future and a hope the Bible says.

To receive Jesus as Savior and Lord of your life, pray:

"Lord, I am a sinner—one who has failed the standards of righteousness You've set forth in Your Word. I believe that Jesus is the Messiah and Risen Son of God. Forgive me of all transgressions. I accept Your blood sacrifice for me. I accept Jesus as Savior. I repent; I turn from my own ways of thinking and acting to Your ways of thinking and acting set forth in the Holy Bible. I set myself to follow Jesus as my Lord."

Next pray for Jesus to baptize you or fill you with the Holy Spirit to receive power to witness and stand for Jesus Christ. Follow Jesus as Shepherd and King through obeying the Bible. Seek fellowship with true Christian believers. To grow strong, give yourself to the Word and prayer just like the first believers in the Book of Acts. Get to know the heart of the Father for you.

ABOUT THE AUTHOR

Delores Roseboro Medley is a minister and writer marked by the love of God. Encounters with God's love date back to age six. Again around age 19, the Lord's love became very real to her. In the early 1980s, Delores experienced the baptism of the Holy Spirit with such fire that she spoke in a heavenly language continuously for three days. Married to Ronnie Medley for 48 years, she has been successful in family life. The Medleys have raised three sons and eight grandchildren. They have two great-grandkids so far. Delores and Ronnie reside in Badin in Stanly County, North Carolina.

Delores has studied at the Rhema Bible Training Center and through the More Than Conquerors Bible School in Charlotte. She is a student now at Life Christian University at Training to Reign in Albemarle.

God's love has informed Delores' ministry in a great way over the years. She served in Aglow International in leadership in Western North Carolina from 1997; she was Area President from 2002 to 2007. Under Aglow, Delores was the coordinator for the Love Your Neighbor Outreach in the mid-Atlantic region. And she was the North Carolina coordinator for Church ~Aglow, a marriage between Aglow and the organized church. Her role in Aglow International is ongoing as she fulfills the call to equip Aglow women for prayer and leadership; she is currently the Vice President of Ministry Development for the Western, North Carolina Area Team. And she teaches at Aglow gatherings.

In June 2004, Delores Medley was ordained as a pastor under senior pastor Darryl Medley at Spirit and Truth United Church of Worship in Albemarle, NC. Today, Delores is the assistant pastor at Spirit and Truth where she leads the anointed "Call to Pray" intercessory meetings. Delores also mentors women one on one; she is a recognized seer. Strong in her heart is a desire for the Body of Christ to know and understand the

Father's love for them and move in higher realms of faith. God's love is the mighty weapon the church possesses to win lost souls. Delores says, "God's plan always involves relationship. First we relate to Him; next we relate to others. 'And this is His commandment that we should believe on the name of His Son Jesus Christ and love one another as He gave us commandment.'" (1 John 3:23) With this aim, the author has produced this book.

Contact Delores Medley

Pastor Delores Medley is available to speak and minister. She brings messages from the heart of God and flows in the spirit of love. God has gifted her to teach the Word. To contact her for speaking engagements in the community, conferences, prayer retreats, and church gatherings, send an email to lovesaim1949@gmail.com. Also, Pastor Delores is available for one-on-one mentoring ministry. Contact her for appointments through the same email.

Delores plans to give away many copies of *Love's Aim* to touch and bless readers in Stanly County, western North Carolina, and points beyond. The plan is to give *Love's Aim* to those without Christ as a witness and testimony to the reality of a God of Love. If you would like to support the free distribution of this book, send offerings to the address below. A shipment of 120 books cost her approximately $495. Any amount is welcome. Thank you so much for sowing love into people through contributing to giving away copies of *Love's Aim*.

Delores Medley
P.O. Box 197
Badin, NC 28009